ENDORSEMENTS FOR
Passionate Housewives Desperate for God

"*Passionate Housewives Desperate for God* is an exceptionally well written book. Jennie Chancey and Stacy McDonald do not pretend to be the perfect wives, mothers, and homemakers, but they do have a heart for God and His glory. Both of them see the role of the wife and mother as God's high and holy calling, and they exhort us through Scripture and practical examples to, by God's grace, fulfill that calling. This book will make you think, will convict you, and will, as the subtitle states, give you a 'fresh vision for the hopeful homemaker.' I highly recommend this book."

—MARTHA PEACE, biblical counselor and
author of *The Excellent Wife*

"Jennie Chancey and Stacy McDonald have spoken the Truth with a capital T in their wonderful book *Passionate Housewives Desperate for God*. Totally grounded in Scripture, this book winsomely presents the true picture of a godly homemaker. Prepare to be stimulated, challenged, and encouraged as a woman. This book is a real gem!"

—VICKIE FARRIS, wife of Michael Farris, founder of
the Home School Legal Defense Association

"Jesus came that we might have life abundant. *Passionate Housewives* reminds us where we might find that life: in submitting to our husbands, in serving our children through loving and training them, and in believing the Word of God."

—DENISE SPROUL, wife of Pastor R.C. Sproul, Jr.

"*Passionate Housewives Desperate* for God challenges women to enthusiastically embrace our high calling—that of wife and mother. Be encouraged as Jennie and Stacy reveal God's truth and expose the lies that lead to disillusionment. May you come away empowered by God's grace to love and honor your husband and to joyfully lead your children by example to love God and serve others."

—MICHELLE DUGGAR, wife of Jim Bob Duggar, whose family story has been featured on Discovery Channel's "Raising 16 Children"

"Hope! Hope! Hope! This book gives hope to Christian women who desire a Christ-centered vocation of victory as wife, mother, homemaker, and woman of God. Jennie and Stacy expose the fraud of Christian feminism and provide practical wisdom for all who aspire to be women of God."

—BEALL PHILLIPS, wife of Doug Phillips, president of Vision Forum

"As a mother of eight, I am encouraged to see this book published to help women who desire to walk as passionate servants, who want to 'do the right thing' and who love the natural yearnings which God created in them. We all have a longing to create, cultivate, and faithfully nurture the gifts God has given us. When the gifts come in the form of family, we would do well to listen to the biblical wisdom of Stacy and Jennie to counteract the Western culture's strident cry for self-assertion. I gladly recommend this book for all women who want to honor Him and help others (even a two year old!) to glorify Him by dying to self with joy and thanksgiving. He is worthy of our efforts, and these two authors cheer us on to biblical femininity."

—VALERIE SHEPARD, wife of Pastor Walt Shepard
and daughter of Elisabeth Elliot

"In an age of constant confusion and conflict over the role of women, *Passionate Housewives* provides a clear-cut message of biblical encouragement and hope for every woman who truly desires to glorify the Lord as a wife, mother, and homemaker."

—CRYSTAL PAINE, wife of Jesse Paine and
founder of BiblicalWomanhood.com

Passionate Housewives Desperate for God

Fresh Vision for the Hopeful Homemaker

By Jennie Chancey
and Stacy McDonald

THE VISION FORUM, INC.
San Antonio, Texas

FOURTH PRINTING
COPYRIGHT © 2007-2009 THE VISION FORUM, INC.
All Rights Reserved

"*Where there is no vision, the people perish.*"

The Vision Forum, Inc.
4719 Blanco Rd., San Antonio, Texas 78212
www.visionforum.com

ISBN-10 1-934554-15-4
ISBN-13 978-1-934554-15-9

PRINTED IN THE UNITED STATES OF AMERICA

Contents

Acknowledgements

We are so thankful for the many people who encouraged us and inspired us to write *Passionate Housewives Desperate for God*. Someone once said that writing a book is like giving birth. Both of us, having been through that process more than a few times, would have to agree. There were those who inspired us, those who helped to nourish the pages, and those who labored alongside us, helping us to "birth" the final manuscript you now hold in your hand. A heartfelt thank you to all of you—both those listed here and those who worked behind the scenes. May God richly bless your efforts.

From Both of Us

Carmon Friedrich of www.buriedtreasurebooks.com, a mutual friend to us both, has been a wonderful source of wisdom and advice through this process. Carmon, you gave us a tremendous gift of time as well as expertise, and we cannot thank you enough.

Mary Alice Burkhead, thank you for your consulting help and being a wonderful example of godly womanhood in the face of extraordinary circumstances and trials.

Marci Putman, thank you so much for clueing us in to the

"Mommy Myth" wars raging on the Internet and for sharing your insights from conversations with other keepers at home whose lives powerfully refuted the unbiblical teachings of "Self First." Your wise advice served us well.

Pastor Tim Bayly, your courageous and biblical stand against egalitarian compromise in the church has inspired many Christians to stand firm. We thank you for your willingness to critique our chapters on feminism as we sought to define terms accurately. Your wise counsel came at the perfect time, and we are grateful for the investment.

From Stacy

Do you remember the classic optical illusion of the old woman and the young woman? At first glance, all one sees is the profile of an old woman with a gnarled expression. But gazing long enough upon the image eventually transforms the haggard woman into a beautiful young maiden. I see the myth of the bedraggled desperate housewife in a similar way.

Feminism presents to us a picture of a haggard household drudge and attempts to convince us this is what serving our husband and children makes us into. For me, it took seeing real godly women living out the truth of Titus 2 with joy and transparency before I was able to gaze through the lens of Scripture and see the reality—that the feminist portrayal was an illusion. Suddenly the beauty, strength, and dignity of the godly keeper at home were revealed to me.

As I look back over my life, I see how God used my wonderful mother, Lorraine Cappel, to instill in me a love for home and everything feminine. She taught me to make a house a home and to honor guests by carefully preparing for their arrival and making them feel special. She trained me to keep an orderly home that would help to create a peaceful, well-run environment. She and my father stressed the importance of family and exemplified a committed marriage and the unified front needed to raise secure children. Thank you, Mom (and Dad), for inspiring me in so many ways.

God's Providence is a wondrous mystery. I am thankful to my Lord and Savior, Jesus Christ, above all others. The year He brought me into the Kingdom, I was twelve hundred miles away from my family, scarred from sin, and lonely. In His mercy, He divinely placed in my life a beautiful Titus 2 woman, Brenda Joyner, who, along with her husband, showed me by their lives a picture of Christ and His Bride. Thank you, Brenda—may your life continue to birth spiritual daughters.

Thank you to the ladies of Providence Church in Peoria (and Karen Riggenbach) for your patience with me as I struggled through the final weeks of completing *Passionate Housewives Desperate for God*. Your advice, input, support, and prayers have been crucial.

Thank you to Janet Billson, Tanya Chapa, Kristen Cormick, Tracy Dole, Loretta Lanphier, Christy Stouffer, and the rest of the Patriarchs' Wives (a private Yahoo email list for women) who inspired me to live and to teach biblical womanhood in the home. Your real-life experiences and stories, as well as some of your fiery discussions on our list, have helped me to flesh out many of my thoughts while writing this book.

To my oldest three daughters still at home, Tiffany, Melissa, and Jessica, your help with the load of extra housework and working with the little ones this last month was the truest blessing of all. In you and your younger sisters, Abigail, Grace, and Emma, I see what I'm writing about. One day you will be godly keepers of your own homes. I pray you will be bright lights dispelling the darkness of feminism and extolling the virtues of true godly womanhood. You are the heroic reformers of the future.

To my daughter, Christa—though you weren't yet married when I began this project, you have now begun your own journey as a passionate housewife and soon-to-be mother at home. Thank you for living out what you were taught to the glory of God—you help make this book ring true.

To my beloved, James, the loving head of our home—the patriarch of our family: Without the support, encouragement, and prayer you offered, this book project would never have made it to completion. You have shown me in living color the picture of a godly servant-leader. Thank you for brainstorming with me, for listening to me rant about the evils of "me-ology," and for being willing to read "just one more chapter, one more time." You are my knight in shining armor, and you give me all the more reason to be "passionate" about being a housewife. I love you.

From Jennie

Jennifer McBride, your heartfelt notes and scriptural exhortations back in February of 2005 spurred me on to pray and think and reach out to the women caught in the crossfire of this debate. Thank you for all your sweet work online and off. I praise the Lord for you.

Acknowledgements

Julie McClay, you gave me a great blessing when you invited my children over to play with your young ones one day in the fall of 2005. That was when I managed to really pull my thoughts together coherently and get this book project started. I am so thankful to have you as a friend—God bless you for that investment in my life.

Keen ladies, you are more than down-the-street neighbors; you are precious sisters in Christ and comrades in arms! How can I thank you for all you have done for our family over the years? You've played with our children, vacuumed our floors, fed our lizard, and put up with our random travel schedule. Thank you for praying for this book project. Y'all are wonderful!

Lydia Sherman, I'm so glad you got in touch with me back in 2001! Thank you for introducing me to Taylor Caldwell's incisive writings on the feminist movement and for continuing to provide encouragement to women all over the world through your fresh, delightful articles.

Mom, I can never thank you enough for all you've put into my life. You've *lived* this book and set an example for me that I pray I can emulate for my own children. I can't say it enough: Thank you, thank you, thank you.

Julie and Heather: You two have inspired me in ways I don't think I can even fully express. As sister and sister-in-law, you have been wonderful friends and such a source of encouragement to me. Heather, thank you for letting us use your experience as part of the basis for the second "Carolyn" story in this book, illustrating how the Lord uses what we consider small things (even child training!) to reach out to others.

To my sweet daughters, Belle and Felicity: You are only

five and three now, but you already love femininity and joyfully embrace it. I so enjoy watching you mommy your baby dolls and set up tea parties on your little table. I smile when I hear you playing dollhouse together and admonishing the "children" to love Jesus and obey their parents. I often feel woefully inadequate when I ponder all that there is to teach you, but I pray daily that God's grace will be sufficient as I encourage you to follow God's plan for beautiful womanhood. You inspire me daily to persevere. May the Lord make you into "corner stones, polished after the similitude of a palace" (Psalm 144:12b). I love you both!

To my wonderful husband, Matt: I can't even begin to tell you how much I love and admire you—more each day! You have been my best friend from the beginning, knowing my faults and loving me through my failures. I thought I loved you when we were newlyweds; I didn't even know what love was. Every year with you is better than the last. What a gift to have you for my husband! Thank you for all the brainstorming sessions and read-alouds and pinpoint comments. Most of all, thank you for affirming me in my role, leading me to seek Christ's kingdom in all things, and picking me up when I fall short. Thank you for eight beautiful children and eleven years of adventure. It has never been dull!

To all the readers of LAF (www.ladiesagainstfeminism.com) who have taken the time over the years to send encouraging words: thank you. I don't think this book would exist if it wasn't for all of you, faithfully and quietly laboring to do the Lord's work without applause or recognition. You are my heroines of the faith.

Acknowledgements

Finally and most importantly, to my gracious Savior, Jesus Christ, Who called me to know Him from childhood and Who rescued me from feminism when I had blinded myself to the Truth. Lord, thank you for reminding me that You "must increase, but I must decrease" (John 3:30).

Preface
Dispelling the Myth
Stacy McDonald

Who can find a virtuous woman? For her price is far above rubies. (Proverbs 31:10)

In the 1970s, the pro-feminist bestseller *Stepford Wives* turned the traditional housewife into a mindless, husband-pleasing, yes-woman who was literally heartless—because, come to find out, she was actually a robot. The message was clear: a woman who faithfully serves her family, loves pleasing her husband, and joyfully takes care of her home (from home) is not a "real person," but a contrived fantasy of her overbearing and selfish husband.

Instead of treasuring women and properly utilizing their gifts, our culture has attempted to discard the beauty and uniqueness of biblical womanhood and create an emotionally androgynous power-woman whose worth is measured only by the degree of her ambition, the shape of her body, and her money-making potential. Rather than women renouncing this affront to their dignity, amazingly, the slaves are demanding their slavery!

In place of the glorious picture painted for us in Scripture of the passionate keeper at home, a hollow counterfeit has emerged—a desperate image concocted and promoted by Hollywood stereotypes, magazine models, and women's self-help books. The rise of the Internet has only added to the confusion. As women have gravitated to the web *en masse*, they have met a flood of men and women of all backgrounds and persuasions propounding conflicting notions of what it means to be a woman. The cacophony of ideas and teachings that today's Christian women must wade through as they contemplate their rightful place in God's created order can be simply overwhelming.

Of course, the challenge of determining the meaning of true biblical womanhood is not unique to our time. While today's women may be bombarded with more media streams than their counterparts of previous generations, biblical femininity has always been an unusual quality. This is what led King Lemuel's mother to observe, "Who can find a virtuous woman? For her price is far above rubies" (Proverbs 31:10). Virtuous women have always been rare, and oh, how precious they are!

Finders, Keepers!

Given the age-old challenge of "finding" a virtuous woman, how are we to unearth the rare jewel of Christian womanhood? How does a woman, or a girl on her way to womanhood, truly understand her rightful calling as a daughter of the King?

The answer is this: that in Christ "are hid all the treasures of wisdom and knowledge" (Colossians 2:3); and He has given us "all things that pertain unto life and godliness" (2 Peter 1:4) in the pages of His Holy Word (2 Timothy 3:16-17). And this includes the mysterious secret of what it means to be a virtuous woman of God—and to be a happy keeper of the home.

The term "homemaker" can be misconstrued, to be sure, so even as we seek to define what a godly keeper at home *is*, we must also uproot the deeply entrenched stereotypes of what a housewife or "homemaker" is *not*—or should not be. In our quest to get to the bottom of this issue, it is critical that we dispel the various myths that have been foisted upon us by feminist propaganda through movies, television, and even billboards—to clear our heads of the cobwebs that can keep us from understanding true biblical femininity.

What a Godly Keeper at Home (Or Housewife) is Not

A godly keeper at home is absolutely not a lesser human being, a mindless robot, or a placid doormat under submission to all men; rather, she is created in the very image of God and of equal worth and value compared to man (Genesis 1:26-28). She is the crown of her husband (Proverbs 12:4), a helper suitable for him (Genesis 2:18). Because she trusts God's wisdom in establishing perfect order for His creation, she willingly submits to her *own* husband as unto the Lord (Ephesians 5:22-24).

In God's economy, the godly housewife is no man's slave or piece of personal property; for her worth is "far above rubies" (Proverbs 31:10). Nonetheless, she eagerly admits to being Christ's slave, which paradoxically makes her free indeed (1 Corinthians 7:22). She laughs when she hears rumors that she is an oppressed victim of a male-dominated dictatorship, because she knows that God's will is perfect and His Word timeless. Her place in society isn't ruled by the culture, but by

God's unchanging and eternal Word. By His grace, she has no desire to question His ways (Isaiah 55:8); on the contrary, she rests in them.

Hardly childish or unintelligent, the godly keeper at home opens her mouth with wisdom (Proverbs 31:26) and her husband and children praise her (Proverbs 31:28). She has opinions and ideas, and uses them for God's glory—not her own. She takes joy in being a helpmate to her husband so that her "husband is known in the gates" (Proverbs 31:23) and so that his heart "safely trusts in her" and he "has no lack of gain" (Proverbs 31:11).

Though the counterfeit lure and charm of the seductress seeks to deceive and entice the housewife's husband, the godly woman's garden is filled with fragrant spices and delicious fruits (Song of Solomon 4:16). As she ravishes her husband's heart, he sings of how her love is better than wine and her scent finer than expensive perfume (Song of Solomon 4:9-10). She is a fruitful vine at her husband's table (Psalm 128:3), and the fruit of her body is blessed (Deuteronomy 28:4).

Far from being a household drudge chained to her stove, the godly keeper at home is like a merchant ship; she brings her food from afar (Proverbs 31:14). Proverbs 31 reveals to us how a godly housewife impacts her community in various ways— feeding the poor, making purchases for the proper running of her household, dealing in wisdom with employees, and selling her homemade goods. She is known in the community and honors her husband by representing him well while in public, yet her hub of productivity and her primary focus is the place she most loves to be—her home.

The godly keeper at home wisely governs the household that God places in her care so that prudence and sound judgment rule her decisions rather than covetousness or folly. Though she may wear pearls and high heels, she realizes that "charm is deceitful and beauty is passing, but a woman who fears the Lord, she shall be praised" (Proverbs 31:30 NKJV).

Desperate Housewives

Still, there are more myths we need to dispel. In this book, we take the long-venerated '50s housewife, wearing high heels and pearls to vacuum the floor, and send her back to the land of fantasy where she belongs. Real women need to know that being helpers to their husbands, raising godly children, and properly managing their homes takes real work, but the rich reward a woman receives by diligently tending to the ways of her household is well worth the effort.

Yet even as the 1950s cardboard caricature of the perfectly polished housewife must be upended, so too must the equally subversive notion of the "desperate housewife" which has made its way into the minds of most Americans.

Hollywood would like for us to believe that a woman who stays home serving her husband and children is not joyful and content, but desperate. Today we have television programs that divulge all the spicy details of what's supposedly going on behind the closed curtains of those seemingly happy housewives. According to modern thought, although she may be smiling when she checks the mail, the cheerful mom across the street lives a life full of secret disappointment, anger, lust, adultery, insanity, and even murder. "Poor, desperate housewife…if only she had a fulfilling career. If only her family didn't drag her down. If only she would do something for her*self* for a change."

This foolish image of sensual despondency on the part of the housewife is a twisted perversion of the beautiful picture of the wise and chaste keeper at home described in Proverbs 31. While every homemaker at times falls short of this scriptural ideal, when the godly keeper at home is faithful, her husband and children rise up and call her blessed (Proverbs 31:28), and her own works praise her in the gates (Proverbs 31:31). The joyful and satisfied life (Proverbs 31:25) that God gives a woman who is surrendered to His will is rich and filling—yes, even passionate!

What Are We Desperate For?

"So, housewives aren't mere drudges or empty-headed arm décor for their husbands," you say, "but you have to admit there is something to this whole 'desperate' thing, right? After all, read the headlines." Yes, there *is* something to it, but not what pop culture would lead you to believe.

Desperation is a condition which is natural to mankind. Jeremiah 17:9 tells us that our hearts are desperately wicked. All of mankind is hopelessly in need of a Savior, and we are doomed to Hell without Him. Scripture tells us that all have sinned and fall short of the glory of God (Romans 3:23). If we claim Christ, then in essence we are admittedly desperate for God. We know that we can do nothing without Jesus and that we can do all things (that He has called us to do) through Him (Philippians 4:13).

Most people don't understand that Jesus Himself was

the perfect model of godly servanthood. How is the world to comprehend His desire for obedient hearts who are willing to serve—not expecting to be served (Mark 10:45)—unless we Christians are showing (not just telling) them we believe it ourselves? As Christian women, we must learn to let Jesus satisfy our souls, for He will do a much better job at quenching our thirst than we ever could. Our attempts to satisfy ourselves will always leave us thirsting for more, never pleased or content—desperate indeed (John 4:13).

If you're feeling overwhelmed and desperate, you won't find the answer in yet another self-help book or in a temporal bottle of pills. More self-esteem won't quiet those inner yearnings or fears any more than a "better" body or new clothes will. Only Christ can satisfy your anxious heart and give you peace. Long for Him "as the deer pants for the water brooks" (Psalm 42:1). When your soul is disquieted, hope in God and praise His Holy name (Psalm 42:11).

An Answer to "Me-ology"

One of the reasons Jennie and I wrote this book is because we know there are "desperate" women who need to hear the truths of Scripture. They need to know about God's wonderful solution to their desperation—and that it won't be met by chasing after more "me time."

Two and a half years ago, when Jennie called to tell me her "hair was on fire" (a Southern term for being all "riled up"), I knew we had to do something. So what was so hair-raising? A friend had alerted Jennie to yet another "me-ology" book—that's how we describe books that encourage women to "pamper," rather than "sanctify" their flesh. Page after page, the author told women it was okay to live for *self*—in fact, if you don't feel like your relationship with God is productive, perhaps it's your family's fault for distracting you from the "important" things you could be doing!

This self-centered philosophy is a fallacy that we as Christian women must guard against. If we find ourselves in a position where we feel that serving our families gets in the way of serving Christ's Kingdom, then we should fall on our faces and repent, because, chances are, if we're not serving the Kingdom, we're serving ourselves—not anyone else.

Serving our family *is* serving the Kingdom. Serving our husband and our little ones is serving Christ Himself—and neglecting them so that we can pursue self interests is neglecting the Kingdom of God—and Jesus Himself! "Inasmuch as you did not do it to one of the least of these, you did not do it to Me" (Matthew 24:45).

Ordinary Housewives Passionate for God

This book represents two and a half years of the work and prayers of two ordinary housewives who are slowly learning to die to self. We haven't arrived yet as homemakers, but we are seeking to conform our lives more and more each day to God's vision for godly womanhood—a calling which we are passionate about, even as we pray you will be.

Here's what we have learned: as we have pried our covetous fingers off those things that are not for us and instead clung to God with all our might, we have found our desperation met with mercy, strength, and power by our loving and powerful Savior.

While it may seem counterintuitive, the lesson is true: living *more* for self will only keep us further from that true joy we're after as women. God wants us to know that we can't do it all, so that He can do it through us—so that He can equip us with the grace and strength we need to accomplish His will—which includes serving Him by serving others. Then, at last, we can shed the millstone of fear and desperation and get truly passionate!

You can call us housewives, homemakers, or keepers at home; but we're not desperate. Whatever challenges God brings us in our role as women, we have purposed to not lose heart or despair. And when we do fall into sin, God graciously reminds us of our utter reliance on and need for His sustaining grace.

Have you struggled to reconcile God's vision of virtuous womanhood with worldly myths that marginalize and mock the role of the homemaker? If so, then we invite you to pull up a chair, dust off the cookie crumbs, and join us as we dispel the mistaken notion that women can and should "have it all." Listen as we share how you can find true contentment in God's Providence—in His holy order—and discover overwhelming joy in the mysterious dichotomy of gaining abundant life (John 10:10-11) by dying to self.

It's time to lay aside the stereotypes and glamorized myths and discover the rare jewel of godly womanhood—to rediscover what it means to be a passionate housewife "desperate" for God alone!

Chapter One

The Other Side of the Street

Stacy McDonald

With a mixture of guilt and irritation, Carolyn looked up from the book that had consumed her afternoon. "What have they done to the living room?" she groaned. A "castle" made of two tablecloths, the baby's blanket, and all of the kitchen chairs met her glance. The once-folded laundry mingled with scattered books and toys around the room. The contents of an entire box of crayons, minus the box, rested beneath the coffee table, and someone's artwork was glued to the electric bill with applesauce.

"I've got to start dinner," Carolyn grumped, feeling more like an unpaid housekeeper than the blissful keeper at home she wanted to become. Glancing bitterly at the clock, she realized her husband, Mike, would be home in less than two hours. "One more page," she thought, as she hurriedly consumed a few more paragraphs.

Hungry for some easy answers to her problems, Carolyn was eager to find out what she could do to relieve her stress and make her family appreciate her. She flipped the book to look at the photo on the back cover. The smiling face of the happy homemaker seemed to taunt her.

"Why is it so easy for her?" she wondered. "Why is it just hard for me?"

"What's wrong, Mama?" a tiny voice chirped from beside the couch. As Carolyn lowered her book, she realized she had sighed aloud.

"Nothing's wrong, hon. Mama's just tired, that's all," she answered her little daughter.

The truth was that Carolyn wasn't just tired—she was restless. She recalled the words of the talk show host from last week: "If you don't make time for yourself, no one else will!" The sympathetic assertion of the Hollywood psychologist's answer echoed in her head, "You can't go through life living for other people."

"Well, that's all I do these days," Carolyn whispered to herself, rising from the couch. "Not that anyone notices."

The discouraged housewife rummaged through the pantry in frustration. She couldn't see anything that would make a complete meal—at least, not quickly. She considered ordering out, then remembered Mike's warning about their finances. Carolyn rolled her eyes and grabbed a box of instant macaroni and cheese.

As she put the pot on the stove to boil, she looked out her window to see her neighbor, Leslie Brown, stepping out of her shiny red convertible. No doubt Leslie's husband was taking *her* out to eat; maybe he even offered to cook dinner himself. She had heard on television that lots of men share the load at home these days! Some men agree that it's only fair to split up the household chores. Carolyn's husband wasn't one of those men.

Carolyn certainly loved her children, and she remembered a time when she truly enjoyed being home with them. What had happened?

She and Mike had married right after college, and both had planned to pursue their personal career goals before having children. However, just as her career began to take off, Carolyn discovered she was pregnant. Mike insisted she quit her job to stay home with the children, so instead of pursuing her own goals, she had left her budding career to be a mom. Her boss and all her colleagues thought she was crazy—even some of her friends at church were amazed. After all, she had such a promising future.

At the time, she had agreed with her husband and was starstruck by the prospect of motherhood and being a keeper at home, but now her eyes filled with tears as she imagined the life she could have had.

She caught a glimpse of her reflection in the mirror above the sideboard: faded jeans, a wrinkled t-shirt, yesterday's mascara smeared under her eyes, hair pulled back in a lopsided ponytail.

"Lovely," she laughed hopelessly.

There was a time when Carolyn had been considered attractive. Now, with the extra weight from the last baby and the fact that she rarely had anywhere "worth it" to go, she had neglected her appearance.

"Why bother? Who would notice anyway?" Carolyn sighed, examining her chewed nails and wondering if her neighbor,

Leslie, got regular manicures.

Carolyn peered through the curtain to watch Leslie unpack her rolling briefcase from the trunk. Her stylish bob bounced as she threw her purse over her shoulder. Her custom-tailored business suit complemented her slim figure. Carolyn listened to the confident, rhythmic click of Leslie Brown's high heels retreat up the driveway to her quiet house.

Carolyn envisaged the interior of her neighbor's home—pristine white walls devoid of fingerprints, shiny floors without crumbs under every chair, sparkling bathtubs with scented bath oils adorning the edge, instead of rubber ducks and squirt toys.

She imagined the peaceful haven Leslie's house must be. Ah, the hush…what she wouldn't give for some peace and quiet! Her daydream was interrupted by the sound of two of the children fighting over something on the second floor.

"Stop it right now, or you're both going to get it!" she yelled.

"What I wouldn't give for the body I used to have, a clean house that *stays* clean, a husband who understands me, time for myself, and peace and quiet—especially peace and quiet!"

Carolyn crumbled on the couch and cried into the cushion. "Why is everything such a mess? My life, my house, my marriage, my children—everything is a wreck! If I'm doing the right thing, then why am I so miserable?"

The peal of the doorbell roused Carolyn from her pity party. All five children ran to the door, clamoring to be the one in front when Mama answered it. Matthew, her oldest, noticed her tear-stained face and looked troubled, "What's wrong, Mama?"

"Don't worry about it, sweetie, I just need a nap." Carolyn

smoothed her hair with her hand, trying to look as cheerful as possible as she opened the front door.

Carolyn's neighbor looked just as sophisticated up close as she had from across the street. She smelled of expensive perfume and was holding a tiny dog.

"Forgive me for bothering you; my name is Leslie Brown. I live across the street. I…I was just wondering if you might be able to help me out. I know you have lots of kids, and I thought one of them might be interested in caring for my dog, Cindy, while I'm away. I'm hoping it won't be too much trouble; she's a very good dog, and I'm willing to pay you."

Leslie seemed anxious, especially since Carolyn had trouble finding her voice right away. Finally, she cleared her throat and answered, "Um, maybe. Why don't you come in? You'll have to excuse the mess. I was just getting dinner started, and I'm afraid the children took over in here."

The two women walked into the living room. Carolyn cleared the couch of toys and offered a seat to her neighbor before sitting down in the faded rocker opposite her.

As Leslie looked around the room, Carolyn wondered what her neighbor must think of her. Leslie sat down while the children gathered around her on the floor, arguing over who would sit closest to the dog.

"Stop the fighting," Carolyn snapped. The children seemed oblivious to the reprimand, and Carolyn awkwardly asked Leslie how long she thought she would be gone. Leslie seemed to ignore the question. "How many children do you have?" Leslie asked.

"I knew it," Carolyn thought to herself. "She's wondering

how many children it takes to turn me into—*this*."

Carolyn looked down at her fingernails, her face reddening. "I have five," she said.

Leslie flashed an amused smile and said, "Really? I can't imagine. You must have your hands full. I never wanted children myself, but I'm glad it works for you."

Carolyn sank back into her chair, not knowing how to reply.

"If you could take Cindy now, I'll pay you ahead of time. She likes ice cubes in her water, and she's afraid of lightning—please don't make her sleep alone if there's a storm." She scanned Carolyn's eyes for sympathy, but Carolyn seemed miles away.

"This *is* going to work for you, right? You can take care of my dog?"

Carolyn took a deep breath and straightened. "Of course we can. My children have been begging for a dog; this will be a good test of how willing they are to do the work required to own one," Carolyn answered in her most qualified voice.

"I'm not cleaning up the poop!" Joshua announced.

"Me, either!" Matthew agreed, falling to the floor and feigning gagging noises.

Embarrassed, Carolyn closed her eyes and sighed. "Boys," she muttered, shaking her head.

She wondered where Leslie would be traveling, but she was afraid to ask. Perhaps she was going on a business trip to Europe. Carolyn had always wanted to travel to Europe. Or maybe Leslie's husband was taking her on a cruise to the Bahamas! Mike had traveled to Italy on business last summer, but Carolyn couldn't go along because one of the children was recovering from the chicken pox. Carolyn pouted inside. Why did Mike get to experience all the excitement and glory in life while she was the invisible helper left to do all the "sacrificing"?

After Leslie left, Carolyn perched on the window seat to check her email on her laptop and do a little surfing on the net before Mike got home. On her favorite Christian blog, she found a great discussion about the freedom women should experience in marriage. It focused on the equality of men and women in their roles as husband and wife. There should be no difference, it claimed. That made such good sense. No wonder she felt so mistreated.

She read as a few articulate and fiery women complained about how men have controlled society—and even the church—for too long. Some blamed the Apostle Paul's patriarchal culture. They lamented the tragedy of brainwashed wives who remain in bondage to their families.

One woman compared biblical submission in marriage to slavery. Women under the unnecessary bondage of male headship will find themselves feeling depressed and trapped. Wives locked up in a house taking care of children all day will rightly feel useless and frustrated because they are living in bondage. "God wants all women to reach their full potential, and if we allow our families to get in the way of our dreams, we will *all* pay the consequences!" they ranted.

Carolyn found herself nodding in agreement as bitter tears ran down her face. She could be doing so much more—enjoying so much more. Why should she be stuck here chasing ungrateful children who won't obey, while Mike enjoys the world? After all, the kids belong to him, too.

Suddenly, the sound of the children playing in the next room was excruciating. If only she had done something important with her life. Mike got to be the "successful" one. She was left home to wipe noses. How could she find fulfillment here, where her potential was wasted?

Later in the evening, after tucking in the children and grabbing a cup of coffee, Carolyn opened the French doors leading to the back patio. She sat in the porch swing and listened to the wind rustle through the trees.

The creak of the swing and the cool breeze on her face reminded her of the night their second child was born. Labor had started while she sat swinging and laughing with her two-year-old. She had been so content then to be home with her "little chickens," as she had referred to her babies. Mike's career was just beginning, and she was eager to see him succeed.

If only she could find a way to change things before it was too late! Perhaps she could actually *be* someone too. She closed her eyes tight, trying to shut out the intruding image of her children in daycare. Her stomach churned as she continued to try to convince herself of the validity of what she knew were selfish desires: *But surely God doesn't expect me to waste the talents He's given me. Some people say children are even better off in a good school than with a mother who is stifled. He wants us all to be happy.*

As much as she had tried, Carolyn hadn't made a very good homemaker. She had read all the books and tried every method and schedule under the sun. Maybe it just wasn't for everyone. Perhaps her talents would be better served elsewhere, and her children would do better under the care of those who were trained to take care of children—experts.

Carolyn wasn't sure what to believe anymore. It seemed the more she considered the unfairness of her lot in life, the more overwhelming her depression became. Nothing but escape sounded appealing. Her eyes burned with tears as the enemy of her soul pointed to the vast array of pleasures and accolades that could have been hers (Matthew 4:8-9). If only she would listen to her heart (Jeremiah 17:9), he whispered, she could be free from all of this drudgery. "What is it?" she cried inwardly. "What am I missing? What's wrong with me?"

Do you relate to Carolyn? Are there times when you feel "desperate" in your role as a housewife? Are you longing for something more in life?

Carolyn had thirsted after the wind (Ecclesiastes 2:17) and was left dry and parched—choking on her own desires.

Are you parched? Do you thirst for refreshment that won't leave you dry and empty, desperate for more? Drink deeply as we journey through God's Word and His beautiful promises for meaningful womanhood. Desperate? Come, learn to be passionate...for God!

Blessed are they which do hunger and thirst after righteousness: for they shall be filled. (Matthew 5:6)

Chapter Two

You Mean It's Not
All About Me?

Stacy McDonald

*For many walk, of whom I have told you often, and now
tell you even weeping, that they are the enemies of the cross
of Christ: whose end is destruction, whose god is their belly,
and whose glory is in their shame—who set their mind on
earthly things.* (Philippians 3:18-19)

Ever since Eve ate of the forbidden fruit that she found
"pleasant to the eyes" (Genesis 3:6) and her husband Adam
followed, man has been absorbed in an undying love affair with
self. God has given us all we need to satisfy our bodies and souls,
just as He did our first parents. Yet we still choose those things
that please *us* rather than please *Him*. Instead of trusting that
God will satisfy us, we continue to attempt to satisfy ourselves.

This narcissistic obsession is an ancient sin we can't seem to
shake. We, that is, Christians as a whole, spend far more time
reading self-help books and listening to motivational speakers
than we do reading God's Word or praying and making our
requests known to Him.

What about Me?

Let nothing be done through strife or vainglory; but in lowliness of mind let each esteem others better than themselves. Look not every man on his own things, but every man also on the things of others. (Philippians 2:3-4)

Many well-meaning Christians want to share with us steps on how we should better serve *ourselves* and remind us of how much more we truly *deserve*, yet God clearly tells us we are to die to ourselves and serve Him by serving others (Matthew 10:39). Also, if we remember that God is just, then we must also remember that because of our sin, all any of us *deserve* is death and destruction. Make no mistake; I'm not endorsing some sort of hyper-spiritual penance of self-deprivation. I'm simply pointing out that, regardless of our trials, not one of us is getting less than we deserve; we're getting abundantly more!

And that he died for all, that they which live should not henceforth live unto themselves, but unto him which died for them, and rose again. (2 Corinthians 5:15)

We can thank the Lord for His inestimable fountain of mercy and goodness and remember that we are not our own; *we were bought with a price*, therefore we must glorify God in our bodies and in our spirits, which are God's (1 Corinthians 6:19-20). We belong to Him—purchased by His own precious blood. Therefore, no matter what He asks of us, it is never too much, and what He expects of us is clear:

This is my commandment, that ye love one another, as I have loved you. Greater love hath no man than this, that a man lay down his life for his friends. (John 15:12-13)

Surely laying down one's life for another, whether physically or conceptually, must cause some sort of pain or loss to the giver. Though some circumstances may seem more difficult than others, we can be assured that God does not take pleasure in our pain, but that He is granting it for our ultimate good and His glory.

I remember once counseling a young woman who was having difficulty submitting to her husband. When I explained to her that Scripture required her to submit to her husband as unto the Lord, she insisted, with more than a little indignation, that it was impossible to submit to a man who wasn't even trying to meet her needs. It was actually his fault, she explained, that she was *forced* to sin by not respecting him.

She went on to describe how her pastor had told her that Scripture didn't require her even to love her husband (ignoring Titus 2:4); only her husband was given that mandate toward her. The neglectful minister also told my friend that she was only required to submit to her husband as long as he "loved her as Christ loved the church." To make it even more confusing, she believed that she was the one who was to decide what "loving her" meant, which in her estimation included (among a long list of other things) how well he fathered their children.

I asked her pointedly, "So, are you saying that you believe you are only required to submit to your husband on the days when he 'loves you as Christ loved the Church?'"

"Yes," she said resolutely. "When he shows me that kind of love, I will have no problem submitting to him."

Her resolve quickly diminished when I pointed out to her that by *her* logic, her husband also would only be required to love her on those days when she submitted to him as unto the Lord. On the days when he viewed her behavior as unsubmissive, he was free to ignore and neglect her. I explained to her that if they both continued to insist on "living for self" rather than "dying to self," neither would ever see success in their marriage. In addition, their children would view marriage as a miserably endless tug-of-war, rather than a picture of oneness played out in life-giving harmony.

Regardless of whether or not our husbands obey the Word, our responsibilities don't change; we are required to obey God by submitting to our own husbands, as the Apostle Peter outlined:

> *Likewise, ye wives, be in subjection to your own husbands; that, if any obey not the word, they also may without the word be won by the conversation of the wives. While they behold your chaste conversation coupled with fear.* (1 Peter 3:1-2)

Thankfully, my friend was more interested in hearing the truth than having her ears tickled. She repented and purposed to submit to her husband regardless of his response or the amount of love and attention he showed her and the children. Her husband eventually came around as he saw the slow and deliberate change in his wife.

She called me excitedly each time he showed some small

gesture of love and affection. However, she knew that she had the responsibility to obey God even when her husband chose to disobey. She was "laying down her life" in love and obedience to God.

It made all the difference in the world in her attitude; she was free to love her husband and family without expectation (Roman 12:10)—and God met her needs.

Desperately Seeking "Me Time"

A popular buzz phrase of the day is, "It's all about you." I have been told that I need to be the one to take care of myself, because if I don't do it, no one else will. Yet the Scriptures teach me that "My God shall supply all of my needs according to His riches in glory by Christ Jesus" (Philippians 4:19).

Many times we're given a long list of things that supposedly all women should have if they are to be happy, refreshed, and satisfied; yet sometimes they have nothing to do with our *actual* needs and don't even resemble real desires we have. I have never had a massage, visited a spa, or had a pedicure. At this point in my life, I simply don't have the time or the inclination; and so far I haven't had a breakdown, and I'm still able to remember my own name (most days).

Please understand there is *nothing* intrinsically wrong with any of these things, as long as we understand that we don't *need* them to be content or healthy and that we aren't somehow deprived if we don't get them. There are many ways we can relax or enjoy ourselves when God gives us opportunity, but to feverishly pursue solace in worldly leisure and personal pleasure is to run to an empty comforter.

In the American pursuit to pamper the flesh, women are told to plan outings where they can spend more time alone (specifically without their children); read books and magazines that make them feel good about what they're already doing; seek out friends who make them comfortable and praise them rather than challenge them; and satisfy their flesh with rich comfort foods and really good chocolate.

Now before you're tempted to assume that I don't believe women should listen to encouraging speakers or eat chocolate, let me assure you that I often benefit from the wisdom of others, especially my husband, the most encouraging speaker I know. I also firmly believe that dark chocolate-covered almonds dusted in cocoa powder should be an option for our daily protein intake and could even be considered medicinal after childbirth.

Again, there is nothing sinful about enjoying the blessings that God places in our paths. My point isn't to convince you that anything that brings you physical pleasure is sinful (Gnosticism[1] is a dangerous heresy), but rather to challenge you to honestly evaluate your thinking. In other words, in your desire for relief from your trials, are you only willing to listen to teaching that makes you feel better about yourself or what you want to be doing, but lacks the power to truly purge the dross from your life?

Do you want to grow in the Lord, or are you content to believe you're fine just the way you are? Are you willing to give up things God wants to remove from your life, or are you attached to material objects and temporal pleasures? Scripture teaches us that we who are Christ's must crucify "the flesh with its passions and desires" (Galatians 5:24). Teaching that has the power to convict and produce repentance and godliness in us seldom feels warm and fuzzy at the time—many times it is, in fact, painful and causes grief and sorrow. As Christians, we must be led by the Spirit of God and not our own flesh, even as the Apostle Paul emphasized:

> *Therefore, brethren, we are debtors—not to the flesh, to live according to the flesh. For if you live according to the flesh you will die; but if by the Spirit you put to death the deeds of the body, you will live. For as many as are led by the Spirit of God, these are sons of God.* (Romans 8:12-14, NKJV)

False Teachers and Modern Self-Help Gurus

> *For when they [false teachers] speak great swelling words of emptiness, they allure through the lusts of the flesh...* (2 Peter 2:18)

False teachers abound who know exactly what women want to hear. Since many of these teachers are women, they know our fears; they know how we fail; they relate to our frustrations; they're acquainted with our temptations; and they are fully aware of what we, in our flesh, *don't* want to do—repent.

> *While they promise them liberty, they themselves are the servants of corruption: for of whom a man is overcome, of the same is he brought in bondage.* (2 Peter 2:19)

If you sin, a plethora of teachers and psychologists will give you numerous reasons why it's not your fault—you can blame your childhood, your lack of self-esteem, your body image, those demanding children, or that oppressive husband who doesn't help out enough around the house. In addition, if you find yourself screaming at your children, don't worry: it doesn't mean you lack self-control or have sinful anger festering in your heart; it just means you need a little more "me-time."

When we invite these spiritual coddlers to our pity party, they are lively and active guests. Full of flattery and sugary promises, they pat us on the back and offer us microwave motherhood—a fast and easy fix essentially void of any nutrition or taste—and, in the end, do more damage than just clogging our arteries. They confuse the thinking and shipwreck the faith of vulnerable women.

> *For the time will come when they will not endure sound doctrine, but according to their own desires, because they have itching ears, they will heap up for themselves teachers.*
> (2 Timothy 4:3, NKJV)

Many of these teachers may claim Christ (some may even be pastors or elders); yet, because they fear that the true teachings of Scripture are too hard for people to bear, they soften and sugarcoat the truth. The result is an ineffectual message, twisted beyond recognition and poisonous to the soul. In an attempt to be popular or more widely accepted, they focus on the pleasant benefits that may come from living a godly life, often omitting the pain and sacrifice that is involved in our sanctification.

> *Nevertheless even among the rulers many believed in Him, but because of the Pharisees they did not confess*

Him, lest they should be put out of the synagogue; for they loved the praise of men more than the praise of God. (John 12:42-43, NKJV)

Beware of Deception

Like all well-planned attacks of the enemy, the intent seems all the more devious when it affects the weak. A young mother who is feeling tired and overwhelmed with her new duties as a homemaker may find comfort in the smooth and deceptive words of the crooning self-help teacher—especially if the teacher claims to be a Christian. A wife whose husband is working too many hours, leaving her alone with the full responsibility of training up the children, might be a prime target for those who would sow discontentment and bitterness in her heart. Remember, the subtle deceivers are the most beguiling (Genesis 3:1).

False preachers, speakers, teachers, and bloggers are ready to tickle our ears under the guise of "freeing" and "encouraging" us. Unfortunately, the only thing we find ourselves encouraged to do from such commentators is sin all the more, and the only thing we are truly free of is the truth. While we're busy navel gazing,[2] other sins are left fermenting in a pool of self-justification. We're left spiritually barren—stagnant—and our lives and our families are rendered ineffective. It is thus incumbent upon us that we watch out for such "counselors," lest we become ensnared:

> *Beware lest anyone cheat you through philosophy and empty deceit, according to the tradition of men, according to the*

basic principles of the world, and not according to Christ.
(Colossians 2:8)

If you have been listening to heathen teachers (television talk show hosts, secular authors, New Age gurus), then you can be certain that somewhere along the way you have been fed error. When we search for scriptural help from strange shepherds, we can be sure the wolves will find us (Matthew 7:15) and lead us into error and heartache:

And He spoke a parable to them: Can the blind lead the blind? Will they not both fall into the ditch? (Luke 6:39)

How do you find out what God's will truly is? Turn back to Scripture for wisdom and truth. Rather than being indoctrinated by the Pied Pipers of "me-ology," allow His holy Word to renew your mind. "And do not be conformed to this world, but be transformed by the renewing of your mind, that you may prove what is that good and acceptable and perfect will of God" (Romans 12:2).

Remember that as a Christian you are compelled to "Study to shew thyself approved unto God, a workman that needeth not to be ashamed, rightly dividing the word of truth. But shun profane and vain babblings: for they will increase unto more ungodliness" (2 Timothy 2:15-16).

Dying to Live

Ever since the day the serpent tricked Eve into "doing it her way" rather than following the plans and commands of God, Satan has been repackaging the same old deception for the rest of us. The enemy of our souls knows that if he can't convince us that God's ways are wrong, he can at least try to convince us that we've misunderstood what God has said. If we would only give up our "unnecessary" convictions, we could have more of the good life, he tells us.

The truth is that biblical motherhood doesn't mean we're promised postcard-perfect days where we lounge together with our little ones on the porch swing in white starched dresses sipping lemonade and singing in harmony. Homegrown children take a lot of hard work—and sometimes "it ain't pretty." Other times, it's breathtaking.

Biblical motherhood means sacrifice, selfless love, and faithful dedication. It means we're there with our families—body, mind, and spirit. To recognize our purpose in motherhood, we must see the godly generations beyond our own children (Genesis 24:60, Deuteronomy 4:9, 7:9). This means denying ourselves (Matthew 16:25) and being consumed with God and His love for us. It means starting each morning on our face in repentance and thanksgiving, pleading for His grace and for the strength to glorify Him in our daily endeavors. It means loving God more than we love our children—and consequently, He will equip us to truly love them and prepare us to serve them through Christ our Lord. It means impacting future generations by our faithfulness now.

We must die to self on a minute-by-minute basis. "Die to self?" you may ask. "What can that mean?" Jesus said that *anyone* who desired to come after Him must deny himself, take up his cross, and follow Him (Matthew 16:25-26). He didn't say, "Of those who desire to come after Me, some will need to take up his cross..." He said anyone. Do you feel like you've been "losing your life" lately? Perhaps you've made the mistake of trying to save it.

We fail to accept the need to deny our flesh and die to self when we're too busy "obeying our thirst." Instead of crucifying the passions and desires of the flesh (Galatians 5:24), too often we go with the flow and listen to the smooth marketers who tell us we desperately need what we don't have—and, furthermore, convince us we need more of what we *already* have.

Since Scripture tells us "it's not all about us"—it *is* all about Him (Matthew 10:38-39)—we can be assured that He will help us to continuously persevere in steadfast service to Him. We must reject the vain philosophies of this world that distract us with selfish pursuits and instead embrace the magnificent paradox of the Gospel. If you feel desperate, are you willing to die—to self? If your answer is yes, then hang on! Because you are finally ready to truly live!

Chapter Three

Embracing Your Sacred Calling

Stacy McDonald

What you do in your house is worth as much as if
you did it up in heaven for our Lord God. We should
accustom ourselves to think of our position and work
as sacred and well-pleasing to God, not on account
of the position and work, but on account of the word
and faith from which the obedience and the work flow.
—Martin Luther

A s keepers of our homes, we've all winced at some form
of the question, "So, what do you *do*?" How many times
have you responded, "I'm *only* a housewife" or "I'm *just* a
homemaker," implying apologetically that you don't *really* work?
The domestic ideology of *Godey's Lady's Book* is long gone, and
the word housewife is more often used as a pejorative than as a
title for the diligent keeper of the home.

Today, even in Christian circles, a homemaker's vocation is
viewed as optional, replaceable, and more like a hobby to fulfill
her own needs than as a vital asset to the family. "You can be a

homemaker, or you can have a career—it's up to you," some say. "It doesn't matter to *us* what you do"—which communicates that what you *do* isn't all that important at all.

Professional Mommies and Disposable Homemakers

More and more women are deciding to stay home with their children and have given up their professional careers, eagerly running to the "experts" for advice on how to be the very best moms they can be—truly "professional" stay-at-home moms.

The well-intentioned professional mother dotes over her children, seeking to be the ever-attentive and educationally focused super-mom. Unfortunately, many times, without a scriptural model, the "professional mom" creates a child-centered home—a fantasy household that is best described as an ultimate playground.

Finally, after spending long days watching dancing alphabet people on television; making organic, fat-free baby food; driving Johnny to soccer; discovering that undisciplined children don't obey; and washing dirty diapers in her marble sink; the exhausted "professional" stay-at-home mom burns out and goes back to work where at least she was appreciated and life was "easier."

But never fear! If motherhood proves too taxing, for a competitive price, you can hire expert launderers, specialized teachers, trained cooks, certified daycare workers, and professional organizers for your household. Who needs Mom? We live in the age of the "professional." Now the mistress of the house can leave all the pesky homemaking cares to a long list of hirelings while she goes off to work and develops her "true" skills—skills worthy of her attention.

Dorothy Patterson, homemaker and adjunct faculty member of the Criswell College, describes her frustration with society's disdain for the home-working woman and its insistence on the replaceability of the wife and mother. Mrs. Patterson points out the amazing double standard:

> Of course, much of the world would agree that being a housekeeper is acceptable as long as you are not caring for your own home; treating men with attentive devotion would also be right as long as the man is the boss in the office and not your husband; caring for children would even be deemed heroic service for which presidential awards could be given as long as the children are someone else's and not your own.[3]

Young women are no longer trained by Mom to run the household because that would rob a girl of the "best years of her life." Daughters of today have proms to attend, beaches to tan on, boyfriends to obsess over, and malls to hang out at. Who has time for learning to run a home—especially when you don't plan to spend much time there anyway?

Being trained for homemaking is truly a thing of the past; a girl who learns these skills is considered old-fashioned and dull.

I was a mother of six children when, after the birth of my seventh, the nurses refused to allow my newborn to come home with me until I had gone through the hospital's mandatory "diaper-changing course." I had to watch a nineteen-year-old candy striper bathe and diaper my infant before I was considered "fit" to take home my own child.

As offended as I was, I came to realize the reason for this ridiculous procedure was that many women today don't know how to provide even basic care for their little ones. They simply haven't been taught. Many are ill-prepared to boil an egg, much less care for a completely dependent infant and run a household at the same time.

"What does it matter?" you may ask. "Why stifle a young lady who wants to do other things? Besides, what kind of training does it take to push a vacuum and wipe a nose now and then?"

This is where we need fresh vision, because our work at home does so much more. Rather than burden the wife and mother at home with a myriad of educational "musts" for her toddler or create a ridiculous picture of a daycare-flavored home life for her to emulate, why not give her a vision for what is real, what is industrious, and, most of all, what is important to the kingdom of God?

The fact that so many Christian women no longer see the depth and breadth of what it means to be a keeper at home is a troubling cultural trend—and it hasn't happened by accident.

The Invasion of the Baby Snatchers

The minimization of the homemaker's role has been a priority of the feminist movement for decades. Feminist advocates have sought to downplay the maternal desires of women and break down the ties that bind a mother to her home and children. French author and feminist Simone de Beauvoir warned her fellow feminists that if they were to be successful in their agenda, they must destroy "maternity and maternity instincts" in women. She went on to say:

No woman should be authorized to stay at home and raise her children. Society should be totally different. Women should not have that choice, precisely because if there is such a choice, too many women will make that one.[4]

Authorized? So rather than be chained to our stoves, as we're accused of being, we'll be chained to our typewriters—or worse yet, we'll be chained to *someone else's* typewriter? I suppose they think that's better, just as long as we're not stuck under our *own* roof. American critic and memoirist Vivian Gornick had similar plans for women:

Being a housewife is an illegitimate profession...The choice to serve and be protected and plan towards being a family-maker is a choice that shouldn't be. The heart of radical feminism is to change that.[5]

So the proponents of "choice" once again want to give us *no* choice but theirs!

Yet even those of us moms who have chosen to go against the grain can still be lulled by feminism's lies. We can be lured by the insidious notion that being separated from our home and little ones is a good thing. We too can become convinced that it's better for everyone if Mom pursues her own interests. I know; it's happened to me.

When my children were small, I remember considering the use of a mothers' day out program at a nearby, local church. I wasn't sure it was the best idea, since I was truly grateful to be home with my children; but our family had just moved, I had a newborn baby, and I was tired of chasing a toddler in the midst of opening boxes and running a home. So the thought of a "break" a few times a week sounded good.

I also reasoned that it might give me new opportunities to "minister" to others—opportunities seemingly lost in the day-in and day-out of mashing bananas and potty training. I considered the various "women's ministries" that were available at the church we were attending and wondered which ones matched the time slot of my newly-discovered hours of freedom. I reasoned that it would be good for my son to interact with other toddlers, learn new Bible songs, and obtain a little preschool style education that I didn't always have time to provide.

So one day, I did it. I took my two-year-old bundle of bona fide boy-power to a Christian mother's day out program. It would be "good for him," I reasoned. And "good for me too," I thought, as I eagerly considered the free time I'd have. As I signed the paperwork, one of the workers looked at my sleeping, eight-week-old angel of a girl and asked, "Will she be staying, too?"

"No!" I answered protectively. Almost immediately a charge of guilt shot through my soul. Why was I willing to give up the "difficult" one, but not my angelic sleeping newborn? As I drove away, I reminded myself that it was only for a few hours. I tried to pretend I didn't hear his cries in my head. Yet after several "play times" at mothers' day out, it didn't get any better. He seemed to know as soon as we drove into the parking lot that Mommy was leaving him here—at this *place*.

One day, as I left the building, I brushed my fingertips on the paper animals on the wall that were entering Noah's Ark and tried to convince myself that leaving him here was a *good* thing. "It's a Christian environment," I told myself. However, as I drove away, the thought hit me, "*What* in the *world* am I doing? This is what I've wanted all along—to be able to stay home with my babies! If I'm not *forced* to send him to daycare, then why would I want to leave him crying in a 'mother's day out' program? What's the difference?"

Deep down, I knew that I hadn't left him in the care of others for my feigned reason of socialization or so that he could enjoy a Christian environment; he received every bit of that at home and more. The reason I had made my choice was plainly and honestly spelled out in the name of the program, "Mothers' Day Out." It was so that I could have a day out—a day off—time for *myself* without the "burden" of caring for my busy toddler.

Almost in tears, I turned the van around, hurriedly parked, and ran back into the church. When I got there, I observed a little girl in a playpen who desperately needed a nose wiping— though nobody seemed to notice. I heard another toddler about my son's age, screaming in a rage over being "locked" in his high chair—he had been "mean" to the other toddlers. One of the teachers told me he was sentenced to the high chair often.

I gathered my little one and headed to the van, never to return. I thanked God for the option that so many women don't have—of being with my children—not being *forced* to leave my precious ones while I worked at a job to support them.

I realized right then and there that feminism's empty charm had tugged on my heart—that even as a Christian woman, I was vulnerable. While I had a "choice" of whether to tend to my home or to seek outside pursuits away from my family, I recognized that I was prone to wander whenever I let God's grand vision for womanhood slip from my mind.

In her book *The Feminine Mystique*, feminist heroine Betty Friedan collected hundreds of letters from women who all seemed to be plagued with a similar "strange, dissatisfied voice stirring within." One woman contacted Ms. Friedan, hoping for answers to her despair. She writes:

> But who cares about a "helpless" lonely housewife's life being wasted away by the kitchen sink. About all the millions of potentialities whittling away in quiet desperation...[6]

What Friedan couldn't tell this woman was that the starvation of the soul she experienced would not be satisfied by the cold bondage of the feminist gospel. The "wasted" life she bemoaned came from living a futile life of sin and hopelessness. She needed a purpose; she needed God's grace to touch her heart and His vision for womanhood to set her free—nothing less would do.

Those "millions of potentialities" she lamented were her *gifts*—gifts that were not meant to be hidden under the kitchen sink any more than they were meant to be restricted to a boardroom. Our Creator has given us women a glorious station where we are to employ and invest the talents He has given us. When we recognize and fully embrace our calling, we are finally free to truly enjoy it; we're able to experience contentment in the uniqueness of our role and achieve overwhelming victory in our homes and lives!

A Sacred Calling of Purpose and Victory

Let us turn back the pages of time so that we may fully understand and embrace the noble lifework to which God has called us...

At the close of Creation Week, God created Adam and placed him in the Garden of Eden. He then gave him a mission: to dress and tend the ground (Genesis 2:15). Afterward, God stated that it was "not good that man should be alone" (Genesis 2:18).[7]

Then the Lord instructed Adam to name all of the animals He had created. Perhaps God gave this task to Adam so that he would realize on his own that "there was not found a helper comparable to [suitable for] him" (Genesis 2:18). While all the other creatures had mates, sadly it seemed Adam was left alone (Ecclesiastes 4:9-11).

But God never intended for man to remain alone (Genesis 1:27). He had a heavenly plan for the expansion of His Kingdom that would include generations of fruitful families continuing from the godly one-flesh union of one man and one woman. So God answered Adam's deep need by creating Eve to be his wife and gave them this holy charge:

> *Be fruitful, and multiply, and replenish the earth, and subdue it: and have dominion over the fish of the sea, and over the fowl of the air, and over every living thing that moveth upon the earth.* (Genesis 1:28)

God could have simply raised up a woman from the dust of the earth—an independent creature who could keep Adam company and even partner with him in subduing the earth by

31

pursuing equal and separate ventures. Yet He instead caused Adam to fall into a deep sleep, and from man's own rib God fashioned his glorious completer—woman (1 Corinthians 11:7-9). When we consider Adam's poetic response when God brought to him his new wife, it seems he understood the magnitude of his gift, "And Adam said, this is now bone of my bones, and flesh of my flesh: she shall be called Woman, because she was taken out of Man" (Genesis 2:23).

Eve was Adam's perfect complement, his crowning glory; she was created for the express purpose of completing and helping him to take dominion of God's creation. They were now one flesh for as long as they both should live (Matthew 19:6)—"heirs together of the grace of life" (1 Peter 3:7).

There is an element of mystery in the way God joins a man and a woman, and yet within this covenant God provides a vivid picture of Christ and His beloved Bride, the Church (Ephesians 5:23-33), and reveals to us volumes about the husband-wife relationship.

In serving as her husband's helper, a wife performs many valuable roles. She is to be his solitary lover (Genesis 2:24; Song of Solomon 4; Proverbs 5:19), his counselor (Proverbs 31:26; 1 Kings 1:16-21), and his closest friend (1 Peter 3:17; Ephesians 5:33). She has the unique honor of mothering his children (Genesis 1:28, 3:20, 24:60) and keeping their home (Proverbs 31:27; 1 Timothy 5:14; Titus 2:4-5). In all of her tasks, she seeks to further him as a man. His work of dominion is her work; she embraces his vision as her own as she promotes and enhances his life pursuits.

Yet even as a husband and wife undertake their dominion

work together, they have different priorities. In the family economy, God has ordained a distinct division of labor between a man and his bride. Though a woman may bring extra income into the household by her various home-based offerings, the husband is to be the primary provider for the family. Through hard work (Genesis 3:19; Proverbs 28:19) and the avoidance of folly (Proverbs 13:18), he must ensure that his family's needs are met. Men who fail to do this are deemed as worse than unbelievers (1 Timothy 5:8).

In contrast, the wife's primary role is that of mother and home-keeper. She is to diligently tend to the affairs of their home (Proverbs 31:27), even as she bears (Genesis 3:15; Genesis 24:60; 1 Timothy 2:15) and cares (1 Samuel 1:23; Proverbs 31:21) for their children. In the Apostle Paul's letter to Timothy, we see that even a young widow, obviously single and free from the commitment of a husband, is not encouraged to be independent or find a singles ministry within the church. Instead the Apostle instructs, "I will therefore that the younger women marry, bear children, guide the house, give none occasion to the adversary to speak reproachfully" (1 Timothy 5:14).

Paul lays out a similar directive in his letter to Titus as young wives are exhorted to "be sober, to love their husbands, to love their children, to be discreet, chaste, keepers at home, good, obedient to their own husbands, that the word of God be not blasphemed" (Titus 2:4-5).

The text of Scripture is straightforward and unequivocal: a woman's duties are to be home-centered, and if we spurn this directive we cause God's Word to be blasphemed (Titus

2:5) and risk bringing reproach upon the body of Christ (1 Timothy 5:14). As families shrink and daycares flourish, we also see the breakdown of the family and the disintegration of the God-ordered home—yet too often we don't recognize the connection.

Still there is hope, for great blessing comes when we allow God to transform our hearts and we walk in accordance with our unique calling. Proverbs 31 tells us that the wife and mother who "looks well to ways of her household" (Proverbs 31:27) will receive praise from her family: "Her children arise up, and call her blessed; her husband also, and he praiseth her." She is a crown to her husband (Proverbs 12:4) and is viewed as a woman of invaluable worth (Proverbs 31:10). Her ministry is her family, and "her own works" praise her in the gates (Proverbs 31:31), even as her husband proclaims, "Many daughters have done virtuously, but thou excellest them all" (Proverbs 31:29).

Being a keeper at home is a holy mission; it is a rewarding duty that we as women are to passionately undertake. As part of our sacred call, we are to wisely build a godly, spiritual dynasty (Proverbs 14:1) by helping our husbands advance seven culture-transforming missions which Doug Phillips has summarized so well:

> The household is the God-ordained seat of *education*. It is the first place where we are to develop and communicate a distinctively Christian aesthetic for *culture*. The home is not to be relegated to a mere place for consumption, but transformed into a powerful tool for *industry* and production. In the household (not the state welfare

agency) we find God's true pattern for multi-generational, covenantal *care*. The home, not even the temple or church meeting house, has always been the God-ordained primary locus for daily *worship*. Our homes not only provide us with a platform to honor God's non-optional commands for one-anothering and *hospitality*, but they were designed to be the most powerful forums for *evangelism* and discipleship in the Christian's arsenal.[8]

Ladies, we have a great and glorious work before us. Keeping the home has been entrusted to us by God. Under the leadership of our husbands, we are to train up our children in the way they should go (Proverbs 22:6); we are to create beauty and comfort within our homes (Proverbs 31:22); and the work of our hands should reflect industry and productivity (Proverbs 31:13-21). We are to worship alongside our children, teaching them the laws of God (Proverbs 6:20) night and day (Deuteronomy 6:6-7). We are commanded to practice hospitality to strangers and friends alike (1 Peter 4:8-9)—sacrificing in love a portion of ourselves (1 John 3:16) to those who enter our homes.

Using our gifts and talents to glorify God in our role as helpers to our husbands, all within the well-choreographed dance of home life, imparts a quiet lesson to a watching world and communicates true contentment in the loveliness of womanhood. It declares "His glory among the heathen, His wonders among all people" (Psalm 96:3) and multiplies generations of those who love and glorify God.

We need not be desperate! With joy in our hearts (Psalm 19:8, 119:11) and purpose in our steps (Psalm 37:23), we can walk confidently in the role that God ordained for us since the beginning of time:

> *Thus saith the LORD, "Stand ye in the ways, and see, and ask for the old paths, where is the good way, and walk therein, and ye shall find rest for your souls."* (Jeremiah 6:16)

Heavenly Hands

A growing number of women are shedding the "desperate housewife" label and gracefully donning their calling with gusto. Homemaker and former attorney Cheryl Mendelson has this to say about her experience in both arenas:

> So many people imagine housekeeping to be boring, frustrating, repetitive, unintelligent drudgery. I cannot agree. In fact, having kept house, practiced law, taught, and done many other sorts of work, low- and high-paid, I can assure you that it is actually lawyers who are most familiar with the experience of unintelligent drudgery...Seen from the outside, housework can look like a Sisyphean task that gives you no sense of reward or completion. *Yet housekeeping actually offers more opportunities for savoring achievement than almost any other work I can think of.* Each of its regular routines brings satisfaction when it is completed...You get satisfaction not only from the sense of order, cleanliness, freshness, peace and plenty restored, but from the knowledge that you yourself and those you care about are going to enjoy those benefits (emphasis added).[9]

Often we don't view our daily activities biblically. We

wrongly believe that the more mundane the task, the less significant it is to God. As difficult as it may be to believe, the hands that tenderly bathe your baby at night are no less holy than the hands that serve you communion on Sunday. Every small act of love to your family—every diaper you change, every meal you prepare, every toilet you scrub, every errand you run, every fever you tend to, each tooth you pull, every moment of undefiled intimacy with your husband—each one is a holy act when it's done as unto the Lord.

Over the years, I have learned that so much depends on my being home—my being available to the needs of my husband and my children. Our older children are wonderful helpers, but they are not "Mom." Our little ones need my attention, training, correction, teaching, reassurance, and boo-boo kissing. Our older children still need me for many of those things as well. But they require Mom's attention in other ways too. They need challenging conversation, scriptural counsel, intimate friendship, and advanced home-training.

My husband needs me to be available in a myriad of ways. I may return phone calls for him, write letters, edit emails, make purchases, run errands, pay bills, counsel and pray with him, and yes—even kiss a boo-boo or two! Husbands need attention, and being available to your husband is crucial to your relationship with him.

A Crown for Him

As wives, we are called to reverence (Ephesians 5:33) and submit to (Ephesians 5:22-24) our husbands. Even "as Sarah obeyed Abraham, calling him lord," so are we to do (1 Peter 3:6). While feminists scoff at this teaching, God's Word describes a wife's place as a glorious honor. The writer of Proverbs explains that "a virtuous woman is a crown to her husband" (Proverbs 12:4). Matthew Henry explains this powerful principle in these words:

> He that is blessed with a good wife is as happy as if he were upon the throne, for she is no less than a crown to him. A virtuous woman, that is pious and prudent, ingenious and industrious, that is active for the good of her family and looks well to the ways of her household, that makes conscience of her duty in every relation, a woman of spirit, that can bear crosses without disturbance, such a one owns her husband for her head, and therefore she is a crown to him, not only a credit and honour to him, as a crown is an ornament, but supports and keeps up his authority in his family, as a crown is an ensign of power. She is submissive and faithful to him, and by her example teaches his children and servants to be so too. [10]

Sarah Edwards, wife to the famous preacher Jonathan Edwards, was a true Proverbs 31 woman and a clear picture of the passionate housewife—the crowning glory of her husband. She frequently offered hospitality to visitors and was not only "innkeeper" to travelers, but she was also "cook, housekeeper, and counselor for any who sought shelter, including young men who stayed as apprentices of Jonathan." [11]

Hardly "desperate," she consistently embraced her calling as "housewife and mother of eleven children in a day when there were no labor-saving devices, except for children old enough to help with the chores." [12]

Jonathan was a brilliant and busy man, and his heart safely trusted in his competent wife (Proverbs 31:11)—so much so that "the care of his domestic and secular affairs was devolved almost entirely upon his wife, who happily, while of kindred spirit with him in many respects, and fitted to be his companion, was also capable of assuming the cares which were thus laid upon her."[13]

Her husband was known in the gates as her own "works" built him up and helped him to be the man God had called him to be (Proverbs 31:23, 31).

Jonathan knew how blessed he was. On his deathbed, his thoughts turned to his beloved bride, and he whispered to those attending him, "Give my kindest love to my dear wife, and tell her that the uncommon union which has so long subsisted between us has been of such a nature as I trust is spiritual and therefore will continue forever."[14]

The Edwards' heritage lives on today. In 1874 nearly five hundred of their godly descendants reunited (Proverbs 31:28) to honor the name of Jonathan and Sarah Edwards. If these families have remained faithful, imagine what their godly number must be today, 133 years later!

Like Sarah Edwards, my good friend Janet—mother of twelve and "granny" to another dozen—has sought over the years to act as her husband's comely crown within their home rather than seek her own acclaim elsewhere:

I have been married to the same man for nearly 34 years. I have kept his home and done his laundry (but not his socks; at least not always on time!) I have prepared his meals, answered his telephone, and run his errands. I have carried, birthed, nursed, and taught his children. I have prayed for them and delighted in them—for they are mine, too!

Contrary to the feminists' promise, I haven't woken up and found that all of those years and all of those tasks were wasted. In fact, I believe more than ever that God is pleased with my servant's heart, and that He is glorified by my nose-wiping, my dish-doing, and my child-rearing.

When I examine my life in Christ, I realize that God has used my marriage and my children to refine my rough edges and make me more Christ-like. How would I have learned patience and trust in a sovereign God, were it not for wayward children? How would I have learned submission, were it not for a husband who did not always see things my way?

So working outside the home would have been more fulfilling? How could having a boss (other than my husband who loves, appreciates, and respects me, who knows my strengths and encourages my talents) have been better? There is nothing more satisfying than working with my husband to raise our children to love and glorify God. I have seen the fruit of my labors in the homes of our married children—as they, too, invest their lives raising their children to love and glorify the Lord (3 John 4).

Jesus made himself of no reputation. He did not seek after degrees or recognition. He was content to stay in a tiny area and minister to a miniscule group of people whom the world viewed as insignificant. Kind of like a homemaker, under the authority of her loving husband, ministering to the children who need her.

The Blessing of a Fruitful Womb

In June 2007, *World* magazine reported that when couples were asked to rank what was most important in marriage from a range of nine options, having children came in eighth. Sadly, "only 41 percent of Americans now view having children as 'very important' to a successful marriage, down from 65 percent in 1990."[15] This mindset is not limited to unbelievers, as many Christian couples fail to wholeheartedly seek the blessing of the womb, at times considering children an encumbrance to other personal goals. Yet this way of thinking has not always been normative:

> In the Scriptures, the concern of godly women was not discrimination in vocation but rather, the barrenness of the womb. Women were not pining away, pleading the Almighty to be priests or prophets. They were praying for the blessing of bearing children.[16]

Non-Christians laugh at the hypocrisy and the inconsistencies within Christendom. Rather than blame the culture, the selfishness of men, finances, legalism, or even "irreconcilable" differences, we Christians should put the blame where God does when He reproves His people—we should blame our own idolatry. "Wherefore should the heathen say, 'Where is their God?'..." (Psalm 79:10).

Though the world's concerns are shifting sand (Matthew 7:27), God's Word is timeless. While children today are considered an expense and a burden, God's Word calls them a reward—a heritage. They are probably the only gift (Deuteronomy 7:13-14) that we no longer desire in abundance. Furthermore, under the leadership of a godly man, children are considered "arrows" aimed against ungodliness:

> *Lo, children are an heritage of the LORD: and the fruit of the womb is his reward. As arrows are in the hand of a mighty man; so are children of the youth. Happy is the man that hath his quiver full of them: they shall not be ashamed, but they shall speak with the enemies in the gate.* (Psalm 127:3-5)

Imagine the blow to the enemy if all Christian families were to embrace the sanctified reward that is theirs and welcome more children into their families—faithfully training them up for His glory—multiplying godly families who "Declare his glory among the heathen; his marvellous works among all nations" (1 Chronicles 16:24).

One of the key reasons God ordains marriage is to bring forth children. The Prophet Malachi asks, "But did He not make them one…and why one?" The prophet's answer: "He seeks godly offspring" (Malachi 2:15).

As mothers, we should view the opportunity we have to bear and bring up children as a high honor bestowed upon us by the Lord, not a lowly burden to endure. We should rejoice that God has created us to bring into the world precious souls who will glorify Him, warriors who will contend with the enemies of God. The blessing that Rebekah's family gave her when she married Isaac ought to resonate in our hearts: "Our sister, may you become the mother of thousands of ten thousands; and may your descendants possess the gates of those who hate them" (Genesis 24:60).

I recently calculated the potential in our own family. If each of my children only bears half the number of children that I have, my husband and I will be blessed with 50 grandchildren. Skip only one generation, and assume my great-grandchildren each have five children, and I've left a legacy of 1,250 great, great-grandchildren! This may seem far off, but this coming spring, we are expecting my own grandmother to hold in her arms her first great-great grandchild!

If we are faithful in bearing and training up our children, by God's grace, over the next few generations, we will see a growing army for Christ—an army that will take dominion of the godless nations of the earth for the glory of God!

He is God, the faithful God, which keepeth covenant and mercy with them that love him and keep his commandments to a thousand generations…And he will love thee, and bless thee, and multiply thee: he will also bless the fruit of thy womb… (Deuteronomy 7:9, 13)

Covenant Care: Ministering to Sick and Dying Loved Ones

We must remember that our families *are* our ministries. The responsibilities we have to our families are not limited to just our children. When able, we have a call to care for our dying loved ones as well as those birthed into our homes. Edith Schaeffer exemplified this type of care for her husband, Francis

Schaeffer, during his last days on earth. In the spring of 1984, after her husband's five year battle with cancer, she was given a choice. She was asked by the doctors whether she wanted him to be cared for in the hospital, or if she preferred to take him home.

Her response to the doctors reflected her glorious mission in life. She said, "I don't want him to be separated from us until he is separated from his body…I don't want him to be absent from me, from his daughters, to be shut away in an intensive care unit for these last days. I want to take him home."[17]

In her book *A Celebration of Marriage*, Mrs. Schaeffer shares how her family quickly created a "sudden garden" in plain view of his bed so that he could see the trees, the flowers, and an old fountain that had been brought from Switzerland. She describes how "the things Fran could view from that bed, inside and outside, brought glimpses of different periods of life. It was a homecoming from four stark white walls into firelight, candlelight, birds of all kinds coming to feed…and music… music flooded the room."[18]

As a godly and creative homemaker and a loving, faithful helper to her husband, Mrs. Schaeffer eased her husband's journey into glory and performed beautifully in the sacred calling God had given her.

Whether it be our aging parents, a sick aunt, a mentally handicapped loved one, or our own husband or children; if we utilize the nurturing skills God has given women and develop the hospitable and merciful nature that becomes a woman of God, we will "extend our hand to the needy" (Proverbs 31:20) within our own households. This labor of love enriches the lives of every family member as well as communicates to the world the worth and value of life that God has breathed into man.

Creating a Christian Culture: The Masterpiece of the Home

Every home has a culture—either good or bad, whether by design or by default. The culture of each home reflects the priorities and spiritual temperature of the household. Whether these priorities are deliberately thought out and explained (or merely assumed), they impact each member of the family, permeating the atmosphere of the home and beyond.

Though the husband is the leader in setting the direction of the home, it is his wife who is called to transcribe his wishes onto the family canvas. Whether it is the way she adorns the walls and furniture, creates pockets of beauty throughout each room, speaks words of kindness to her little ones, or fills the air with glorious music—day by day, a woman helps form the aesthetics and character of the home through the fruit of her labors.

Building a rich and vibrant family culture takes time. It takes initiative and perseverance. There will be seasons when a wife's "culture-building" activities will be dominated by a steady stream of diapers and dirty laundry. Yet we must not miss the significance of these menial tasks—for they can be compared to the broad brush strokes upon a grand masterpiece.

The home is a place where memories are made, meals are shared, truths are learned, stories are told, and lives are formed and defined. It is a place of industry and usefulness; a place where thousands of cultural expressions are conveyed and where a family's unique flavor and character are cultivated.

Centuries applaud the great works of the masters. Brilliant artists like Rembrandt, Van Dyck, and Vermeer sometimes labored years to create a single masterpiece. So, too, it takes years to build a masterpiece in the home.

If the world can convince us to acquire a taste for the futile blandness found in a self-centered marriage, to be content with recreational motherhood, and to prefer a sterile, disposable version of home "economics," then we will miss the beauty and poetry that is ours in the heavenly *magnum opus* of a God-glorifying, well-ordered home.

So, as women, we must reject this vain imposter and instead embrace the magnificent feminine artistry of godly womanhood. We must daily sculpt our children into Kingdom treasures (Psalm 144:12) and use the culture-building palate of the home to create a breathtaking masterpiece that spans generations.

The profound impact that a solid marriage, familial love, and godly order has on the children in a Christian home is dramatic. It can mean the difference between life and death, godliness and wickedness, barrenness and the continuance of a godly heritage. As we train up our children in the way they should go—when we rise up and when we lie down (Deuteronomy 6:7), their souls are being nurtured and shaped for His glory (Proverbs 22:6). When God ultimately reveals Himself to them, their habits and manners will be untainted, sharp, and ready to fully embark on a life set apart for Him—a life which causes the Enemy of God to shudder (Psalm 102:15). As we train up and disperse a growing army of godly seed, our "arrows shall be as of a mighty expert man; none shall return in vain" (Jeremiah 50:9).

Submitting to our husbands, loving our families, keeping our homes, walking in sobriety and wisdom, and caring for the everyday needs of others, all within the realm of God's divine order, communicates Christ—and this celebration of family, hospitality, and children causes the world to look upward. By living out our lives in a way that truly glorifies Him, an unbelieving world will be able to say, "Where does that kind of love come from? What kind of God do you serve?" And we can answer in truth, "We serve a mighty and powerful God!" God's name should be exalted in the way we live out our lives— however simple or mundane it may seem. "'The nations shall know that I am the LORD,' says the Lord GOD, 'when I am hallowed in you before their eyes...'" (Ezekiel 36:23).

Christian women must reject any distorted view of the modern housewife—whether it be the miserable household drudge; the fanatical, sock-matching wonder-woman; the child-centered, worn out soccer mom; or the deceptive, apron-wearing vixen. When we consistently renew our minds by absorbing Scripture and by passionately embracing the sacred calling God has truly given us as women, we will refute the perverted image of the desperate housewife by believing His promises and showing the world there *is* something better for which we can truly be passionate!

Chapter Four

Weary Women

Stacy McDonald

He gives power to the weak, and to those who have no might He increases strength. (Isaiah 40:29)

Has anyone ever said to you, "You sure do look tired; you need to get more rest"? Maybe some well-meaning friend has patted your back and told you about your *need* for more time to yourself without the children, so that you won't have a breakdown or wear yourself out. Perhaps they've insisted that, to be truly spiritual or godly, you must have a "quiet time" early each morning in peaceful solitude with the Lord. To top it off, they've probably warned you that if you don't do all these things (that are practically impossible for a mom with young children), you won't be able to take care of your family properly, your relationship with God will suffer, and you may even wind up on the five o'clock news!

Rather than getting angry or frustrated by these statements, we need to know how to respond to them. Even more importantly, we need to know how to rely on God to relieve our burdens—His ways never fail us! In this chapter we'll discuss several ways we can let go of some of the ways we burden *ourselves*, as well as learn how to properly manage the challenges and trials God sends us for our good and His glory.

The Highly Revered "Quiet Time"

I'll let you in on a little secret. I don't have a personal quiet time every morning that is actually *quiet* or *alone,* nor do I know anyone with more than two children who does. Spending time with God and in His Word is crucial, but don't set yourself up for disappointment by expecting a regular time of peaceful bliss in prayer and quiet solitude.

I believe that one of the heaviest burdens well-meaning Christians place upon the shoulders of mothers at home is the mandate of "quiet time."

One mother shared with me how heavy a burden this was for her to bear:

> I have heard over and over that I should have a quiet time every morning. I have felt so guilty over the past four years. I tried everything to have one. Getting up earlier did not work, as I have a little one who seems to know as soon as my eyelids open in the morning. The only thing that happened in my efforts was that I felt guilty and lost more sleep than one already does with little ones.

Another woman voiced her frustration over being told she should get up earlier, sacrificing her already limited sleep in order to have a quiet time:

I am a mother of three boys, ages five and under, and one on the way. I can't tell you how frustrated I get when women from church tell me I just need to wake up earlier or try harder to have a quiet time.

I wake up at four-thirty every morning to see my husband off to work. After he leaves, I try to rest for another half hour before I'm up for the day. Quite often, I forego a shower in order to keep the level of chaos down in the morning. How much earlier do they want me to wake up, or what else besides personal hygiene can I sacrifice?

Moms of little ones need their sleep! We can certainly discipline ourselves to go to bed early enough so that we can wake up with our little ones (or our husband), but to beat ourselves up over our failure to create a worship time that resembles someone else's isn't necessary and can sometimes be detrimental.

It is vain for you to rise up early, to sit up late, to eat the bread of sorrows; for so He gives His beloved sleep. (Psalm 127:2)

Another lady shared how she felt like she was less of a Christian for praying during the short moments God provided during the day:

Our oldest is sixteen, and we have a beautiful, new six-week-old blessing. I know only too well about crying out to God in the middle of the night in exhaustion. I have felt so defeated and inadequate. I can hardly remember a time when I didn't think I was a terrible mother and Christian because I didn't have this "set apart" quiet time with God. Somehow I thought I was less of a Christian to pray in the van or at the grocery rather than at six o'clock a.m.

Rain on Your Despair with "Prayer Droplets"!

Too many women are in bondage to the man-made myth that *everyone* should pray in one great big gush early each morning. But rather than praying a river at an appointed time every day, I would suggest a more reasonable and feasible option for a busy mother: pray in "droplets" throughout the day. Not only is this achievable, it is biblical. We are instructed to "pray without ceasing" (1 Thessalonians 5:16-18) and to let our souls follow close behind Him as His right hand holds us up (Psalm 63:8).

What better way to follow close behind Him than to read snippets of Scripture and pray in droplets throughout the day? As you care for your children, interact with neighbors, and chat with store clerks, "let your tongue speak of His righteousness and of His praise all the day long" (Psalm 35:28). God is your refuge—make clinging to Him every moment become a disciplined habit, even as others look on:

> *I have become as a wonder to many, But You are my strong refuge. Let my mouth be filled with Your praise and with Your glory all the day.* (Psalm 71:7-8, NKJV)

When all your children are small, it can be nearly impossible to even go to the bathroom alone, much less enjoy a half-hour of prayer and contemplation in heavenly, uninterrupted bliss; so get creative! Copy chapters of Scripture or buy small pocket Bibles and place them around your house—in the bathroom, in the laundry room, next to the chair where you nurse the baby—wherever you might have a moment where you're standing (or sitting) still. You'll find yourself rising above your trials by God's sustaining hand when you make His Word a continuous presence in your day (Psalm 119:116-117).

If you have little ones, accept that this is your "noisy season" of life. You'll have moments for "quiet" time later. Pray in droplets during the day as well as when you're awakened at night:

> *Yet the LORD will command his lovingkindness in the daytime, and in the night his song shall be with me, and my prayer unto the God of my life.* (Psalm 42:8)

Pray with your children, pray when you're bathing the baby, and pray in the shower—but pray!

Make Room in Your Prayer Closet for Your Children

Looking back to the days when all my children were young, and I desperately sought time alone with God, I recall thinking, "What's wrong with me? Why does everyone *else* seem to have it all together, and I can't seem to have a single *quiet time* without getting frustrated over being interrupted every five seconds?" I thought I had to spend time with God a certain way for it to "count."

Then there were the mornings when I sacrificed the extra rest and tried to get up *before* the children did. Inevitably, I would open my Bible, begin praying, and then hear the footsteps of a toddler plodding down the stairs. "Mommy, I'm hungry." And so my day would begin in frustration and heaviness without having accomplished my "spiritual time of rest and quiet communion with God."

Rather than pouring some cereal and reading my Bible with the children while they ate and I sipped a cup of coffee, I would begin my day feeling like a failure, being short with the children—perhaps even secretly feeling like God was unfair. After all, I just wanted to spend time alone with *Him*; why couldn't He have kept everyone asleep? I wound up getting angry because I was trying to meet God each day "my way" rather than His, and it wasn't working.

It took me a long time to realize that I needed to serve God right where He had placed me—and I didn't have to be in seclusion to spend quality time with Him. I was in His presence with every diaper I changed, every Bible story I told my children, every meal I prepared, every toilet I cleaned, and every math paper I graded. I learned to gather my little ones around me to pray the Lord's Prayer, for my good as well as theirs.

Besides our time of family worship led by my husband in the mornings, my children and I prayed together, sang together, and studied God's Word together in our homeschool during the day. These times were not any less important or spiritually fulfilling than a quiet time alone. If this is your season of little ones, find ways to include them in your spiritual life.

When reading your Bible, don't get frustrated when you're interrupted right at the "good parts." Learn to view those inevitable moments of interruption as teaching opportunities planned by God. Say to your two-year-old, in your most animated voice, "Joshua, you came at just the right moment; listen to this, 'These things I have spoken unto you, that in me ye might have peace. In the world ye shall have tribulation: but be of good cheer; I have overcome the world' (John 16:33). Isn't that great? Jesus gives us peace in Him! He has overcome the world!" Your toddler will probably laugh and clap his hands in response to your excitement, then he may head to his nearest stash of blocks, but you have had the chance to let God's truth sink into your own soul as well as that of your little one.

Sometimes we get too spiritual for our own good. Jesus was certainly just as holy when He washed the feet of His disciples and healed the sick as when He prayed in the Garden of Gethsemane. Even during the few times Jesus left the crowds behind to commune with the Father, He was often moved with compassion to turn back and minister to them. Christ never snapped at those who cried out for Him; He didn't rebuke them for taking away His "quiet time." Sometimes, He prayed aloud right in the middle of those He had come to serve (John 17). He came to reach out His hands selflessly, and we're to emulate Him.

God will provide us with the rest and refreshing we need. He will even provide us with moments alone with Him at times. But we're not to knock ourselves out trying to get away from everyone to meet with God. We need to learn to find Him in the commotion of everyday life. We must view serving our families as acts of service to God, rather than as acts that "get in the way" of serving Him. Martin Luther wrote about this very idea:

> [Christian faith] opens its eyes, looks upon all these insignificant, distasteful, and despised duties in the Spirit, and is aware that they are all adorned with divine approval

as with the costliest gold and jewels. A wife...should regard her duties in the same light, as she suckles the child, rocks and bathes it, and cares for it in other ways; and as she busies herself with other duties and renders help and obedience to her husband. These are truly golden and noble works.[19]

Sweet Sleep and Sacred Rest

Sleep is important, and we should welcome opportunities for rest, but sometimes God has not allowed for us to have as much sleep as we think we need. If you are the tired mom without any outside help, the faithful mother who is teetering under the weight of sleepless nights and a challenging schedule, be encouraged! Pray and trust God, knowing that He is in control. Be assured that neither your efforts nor your tears (Psalm 56:8) have gone unnoticed by our wise, good, and powerful God; and that He has ordained your steps (Psalm 16:7). Go to Him; plead for His strength and mercy (Psalm 86:16). He will give you the rest needed to accomplish His will, as He promises:

> *Come to Me, all you who labor and are heavy laden, and I will give you rest. Take My yoke upon you and learn from Me, for I am gentle and lowly in heart, and you will find rest for your souls. For My yoke is easy and My burden is light."* (Matthew 11:28-30)

I remember one night praying fervently (after the baby had been up twelve or thirteen times), "Please God, please, please, please let him sleep." And then I heard the inevitable scream. I cried into my pillow because I knew it was only an hour before I had to get up. Wasn't God listening?

So I pulled him into bed with me to nurse, quieted his fretful wails, and drifted off to sleep one more time, desperately hoping for just a "few more minutes" of rest. Yet as if in a dream, I heard the distant voice of one of my older children, "Mom... Mom, Melissa's throwing up."

It was true. Sleep was not meant for me that morning. But I had a choice: I could be bitter toward the family God had called me to serve, or I could ask God to give me the strength I needed to die to self and glorify Him. At the end of that day, though I was physically tired, I marveled how I had made it through and was able to see ways God had eased my burden and refreshed my soul. I was able to nap when the baby rested later in the afternoon, a friend had made an "extra" casserole and wanted to know if I wanted one, and my time seemed to be multiplied—I was shocked at how much I had accomplished. When we trust God, take our eyes off our troubles, and simply choose to do what needs to be done, God blesses us.

Your burdens will seem lighter as you allow Him to carry you. The hours of sleep may not always be the number you would choose, but they will be enough—He always gives us enough. Give thanks to God for His provision, for the life He has given you, and for the family He has entrusted to your care.

Remember, this season of caring for little ones is fleeting. When we are in the midst of diapers, minimal sleep, and challenging days of training, it sure doesn't seem like it, but it's true! Relish these precious moments—remembering this too shall pass.

For our light affliction, which is but for a moment, is

working for us a far more exceeding and eternal weight of glory, while we do not look at the things which are seen, but at the things which are not seen. For the things which are seen are temporary, but the things which are not seen are eternal. (2 Corinthians 4:17-18)

If you are faithful in the early stages of training, your children will soon grow into blessed little helpers. It won't be long until they can bathe themselves, help with meals, pitch in with daily chores, and even help with younger siblings.

As our children grow in wisdom, we do, too. Remember that God is using these trials to do a work in us; to finish what He began. God is faithful, therefore I am "confident of this very thing, that He who has begun a good work in you will complete it until the day of Jesus Christ" (Philippians 1:6).

The Great Satisfier of My Soul

Whenever I'm exhausted and weak and feel the alluring pull of self-pity tugging at my soul, I think of the Apostle Paul. Surely, his sufferings for Christ were many. Aside from being stoned, beaten with rods, imprisoned, starved, shipwrecked, and whipped, he also knew "weariness and toil" and "sleeplessness" (2 Corinthians 11:27). Although he didn't glory in his sufferings, he did glory in the grace of God that enabled him to endure them. I realize my puny trials pale in comparison to Paul's, but it reminds me that even in the worst of circumstances, God is faithfully there to enable us to be more "abundant in labors" and endure even the greatest of sufferings. Focusing on Christ and the grace He willingly gives enables me to rest in Him.

In contrast, if I focus on the things I'm *not* getting because I'm serving my family, and then I'm told I urgently "need" those things, I might easily become embittered against the very people God has called me to sacrificially love and serve. If I strive for a "me-centered" life while I am surrounded by a family who needs me, then I will find myself frustrated and desperate indeed—with an emphasis on despair.

Some days are draining, but we need to let Jesus be the satisfier of our souls. "Blessed are those who hunger and thirst for righteousness, for they shall be filled" (Matthew 5:6). God isn't leading us into a slavish life of misery and hopeless servitude. I'm not a slave of man. I'm a slave of Christ. "He who is called while free is Christ's slave" (1 Corinthians 7:22). So, because I am not my own, but I am bought with a price (1 Corinthians 6:20), I willingly give myself to God and to whatever He calls me to do, and in return He gives me peace and joy—and eternal life.

If we try to satisfy our own souls, we'll just wind up thirsting all the more. Go to Jesus with your needs; go to Jesus for that satisfying drink. "Jesus answered and said to her, 'Whoever drinks of this water will thirst again, but whoever drinks of the water that I shall give him will never thirst. But the water that I shall give him will become in him a fountain of water springing up into everlasting life'" (John 4:13-14).

God will meet needs you didn't even know you had and give you all the rest and refreshing you require. It may come in the form of housecleaning help from a friend, a night alone with your husband, or a meal from someone at church. Or it may be the supernatural rest that only God can give. But, we also need to accept a "no" from God at times. Sometimes it is in the midst of our trials that we gain the sweetest refreshing of all. He will multiply your strength in His own way. The key is to seek Him first, rather than as a last resort. He will give you all you truly need:

> *But seek first the kingdom of God and His righteousness, and all these things shall be added to you.* (Matthew 6:33)

If I trust God and focus on pouring myself out as a drink offering to the Lord by serving others, I do more than believe that He is not going to give me more than I can handle—I believe He is going to equip me to handle what He chooses to give me, because I am called according to His purpose: "Who has saved us and called us with a holy calling, not according to our works, but according to His own purpose and grace which was given to us in Christ Jesus" (2 Timothy 1:9).

Help, I'm Drowning!

Many times we bring frustration on ourselves in the form of too many projects, plans, and misplaced priorities. Remember that God has given you your husband to lead and protect you. Go to him and seek his counsel. Most times he will be able to see things more objectively than you. Perhaps he can help you work out a doable schedule without all the emotions, false guilt, or hormone fluctuations that may cloud the decision-making process of a tired mom. Remember that God works through our submission for our good as well as for the good of our husbands. Don't decide before asking him that "he won't have the answer." Trust that God will work through him. While we learn to trust, our husbands learn to lead.

Use good judgment in managing your activities and your resting time. Often we have grandiose aspirations for all we think a mother should be accomplishing. You don't need to accomplish it all this week—or even this year.

Ask your husband to help you say no to outside activities that would overwhelm you. Perhaps there are times when he even needs to say no *for* you. I know so many moms who run themselves ragged with numerous sports and church activities, play groups, and various children's clubs or field trips. Sometimes the best thing to do is pull the plug on all of it! From time to time, it is vital to stop and reassess priorities and projects. Often, to our chagrin, we'll find that we're bringing undue stress upon ourselves and leaving no time for the restful, un-harried times we need as a family.

There are times when I have had trouble telling people no because I see they really need assistance. This is where my husband can help by guarding my time and protecting our household from too much outside activity. He knows if I really have the time and energy to participate. If something is causing you too much stress, your husband will know it, and he may be the answer to your prayer for help.

The Harder They Fall

Pride goeth before destruction, and an haughty spirit before a fall. Better it is to be of an humble spirit with the lowly, than to divide the spoil with the proud. (Proverbs 16:18-19)

Sometimes our stress comes from a fear that we're failing at motherhood. Perhaps we fear that our children will never learn to read, maybe we agonize over the thought of them rejecting the faith, or—horror upon horrors—we worry they'll disobey us in front of the missionary family that comes to visit! Sometimes our stress and fears are undoubtedly brought on by our own sinful pride.

When I was younger, pregnancy was a breeze. I remember being puzzled over why anyone would complain about something as exciting and effortless as pregnancy. My first baby didn't even bring morning sickness, so the few slight waves of nausea I supposedly "endured" gave me a mistaken sense of self-admiration. "What was everyone *whining* about anyway?" I thought, in my bubble of prenatal arrogance.

However, as my body aged, and I continued to have children, each pregnancy became less and less *fun*. I still loved the end result (the babies), but I heard myself complaining about the very things I used to smugly misjudge in others.

As the pregnancies added up, so did the moments of nausea. No simple "morning" sickness for this "whiner"—24-hour sickness is more like it! And let's not leave off fatigue, sore muscles, aching hips, and a throbbing back. During the second half of my last few pregnancies, I was forced to be off my feet because the varicose veins in my right leg swelled so badly that I could hardly bear it. My skin felt like it was on fire and turned a ghastly shade of purple.

To keep myself from screaming out in pain, I was compelled to wear torturous medical-grade support hose that took me (with my husband's help) fifteen minutes to get on each morning. And as for me and my "I can do it myself" attitude, I was resigned to go on outings riding in a wheelchair with an attachment that elevated my right leg. I assure you, it was a most humbling experience, especially the day I tried to regain a little control by using one of the electric numbers they provide in the stores now. Everything was fine until I knocked over an entire display of canned goods.

Worse than that, I was sure that everyone we passed in the grocery store was shaking their heads at me—the *lazy* pregnant woman who made her poor husband push her through the aisles. "Little do they know," I thought, "but, my husband loves it. I'm the one who hates it!" Normally, he doesn't care to grocery shop with me, because he says I take too long reading labels. He likes to get in and get out. This was his moment of victory; just as I would begin to read "mono sodium glu…" off he went to the next aisle, with my hair blowing in the wind!

I was especially self-conscious when we passed *young* pregnant women. "She's rolling her 22-year-old eyes behind those trendy little sunglasses," I told myself. "She thinks I'm just riding in this wheelchair because I'm lazy and whiny." I continued my inner complaining, "Of course when she gets 'old' like me, she probably won't be having babies anymore."

I moaned and groaned inside, grumbling at the unfairness of it all. Then one day I snapped—I realized that because of my own sinful pride toward others in the past, I was making assumptions about what others must be thinking of me now. When I was young, and things were easier, I compared my circumstances to the circumstances of others and pridefully assumed their trials must be identical to mine—only I presumed my stamina was somehow superior to theirs. Looking back, I cringed at my conceit. The irony of it was that when God humbled me and allowed me to finally go through the same trials I had wrongly judged in others, I once again made false assumptions—but, this time I projected my past arrogance on them.

I was distressed at my sinful pride and amazed at how it had generated my own misery. As I contemplated this scenario in the writing of this book, I realized that perhaps we do something similar when we are embarrassed by our children's poor behavior in front of others. It's very easy to compare our children to the children of someone we admire and become dissatisfied and frustrated with our little ones. This is especially true if we've been guilty of judging the parenting skills of those whose children misbehaved in our presence.

We must remember that when we view other women—other families—we are only outsiders looking in at the part of life they're willing to show us. Or perhaps, in the case of the unfortunate parent with the "crashing and burning" toddler, we see them on a bad day. We can only see a small percentage of what real life is like for them. We can't see the whole picture, nor are we invited to. Our own families and our own lives should keep us plenty busy without the need to speculate about the ups and downs of others.

When we find ourselves anxious over all that needs to be done and focusing on how tired and overwhelmed we feel, we would do well to remember the words of the Prophet Isaiah:

He giveth power to the faint; and to them that have no

might he increaseth strength. Even the youths shall faint and be weary, and the young men shall utterly fall. But those who wait on the Lord shall renew their strength; they shall mount up with wings like eagles, they shall run and not be weary, they shall walk and not faint. (Isaiah 40:29-31)

He Leads Those with Young

Remembering God's mercy towards me lifts from me the burden of frustration and puts things into perspective. Instead of leaving me bitterly longing for more, I am able to rest gratefully content.

If I say, "My foot slips," Your mercy, O Lord, will hold me up. In the multitude of my anxieties within me, Your comforts delight my soul. (Psalm 94:18-19, NKJV)

His mercy is a comfort and delight to my soul; it calms my fears and anxieties. I love to remember that Jesus is my faithful and strong shepherd, carrying me in his bosom, and gently leading me and my little ones:

He shall feed his flock like a shepherd: he shall gather the lambs with his arm, and carry them in his bosom, and shall gently lead those that are with young. (Isaiah 40:11)

There is no place more precious than in the arms of the Father; yet so many times we fight and scratch to be set down on our own. In our stubborn independence, we suppose that only the *big* problems should be brought to God; we imagine that we can handle the daily grind ourselves. As the everyday stress and trials of life erode our strength as well as our patience, we become weak and discouraged. God knows and *understands* our weaknesses (Hebrews 4:15) and is not disconnected from our cries for help. He genuinely loves us and is there beside us!

Perhaps we fear that God will weary of our many complaints, and we hope to ensure His availability by grinning and bearing it in case things get *really* bad. But we need to remember that God does not reason or grow weary the way we do. He has told us to cast our cares (no matter how trivial) upon Him:

> *Therefore humble yourselves under the mighty hand of God, that He may exalt you in due time, casting all your care upon Him, for He cares for you.* (1 Peter 5:6-7, NKJV)

Whatever our reasons are for failing to turn to God on a daily basis, they leave us with the same awful results—anger, guilt, frustration, and weariness. You know what they say: "When life brings you to your knees, it's a good time to look up," showing our tendency to call upon God only in the very worst of times. The biggest problem with that old adage is that it fails to express the necessity of *staying* on our knees. We should have an attitude of humility and a spirit of longing toward God and His mercy at all times. His faithfulness is why we have hope! Jeremiah clung to this promise in the midst of his weary lamentation:

> *This I recall to my mind, therefore have I hope. It is of the Lord's mercies that we are not consumed, because his compassions fail not. They are new every morning: great is thy faithfulness. The Lord is my portion, saith my soul; therefore will I hope in him. The Lord is good unto them that wait for him, to the soul*

that seeketh him. (Lamentations 3:21-25)

As we renew our minds with God's Holy Word and determine to have an attitude of serving others (with Christ as our example), and as we turn to the Lord for our comfort and refreshing, we will find our thirst quenched, our joy made full, and our strength renewed to tackle the next task ahead.

Don't fret over what's to come; just faithfully take the next step. To quote an old English poem Elisabeth Elliot loved to reference, just "do the next thing." Keep your eyes off others; keep them on God, and He will sustain you through it all.

Do the Next Thing

At an old English parsonage down by the sea,
There came in the twilight a message to me.
Its quaint Saxon legend deeply engraven
That, as it seems to me, teaching from heaven.
And all through the hours the quiet words ring,
Like a low inspiration, *do the next thing.*

Many a questioning, many a fear,
Many a doubt hath its quieting here.
Moment by moment, let down from heaven,
Time, opportunity, and guidance are given.
Fear not tomorrows, child of the King,
Trust them with Jesus, *do the next thing.*

Do it immediately, do it with prayer;
Do it reliantly, casting all care.
Do it with reverence, tracing His hand,

Who placed it before thee with earnest command.
Stayed on Omnipotence, safe 'neath His wing,
Leave all results, *do the next thing*.

Looking to Jesus, ever serener,
Working or suffering be thy demeanor;
In His dear presence, the rest of His calm,
The light of His countenance, be thy psalm,
Strong in His faithfulness, praise and sing.
Then, as He beckons, *do the next thing*.

Author Unknown

Chapter Five

Too Good To Be True: Freedom from the Bondage of Perfectionism

Jennie Chancey

For we all stumble in many things. If anyone does not stumble in word, he is a perfect man, able also to bridle the whole body. (James 3:2, NKJV)

Somewhere along the line, we've bought into the strange idea that Christians are supposed to appear to be perfect people—people who do not make mistakes. True, God declares that we are to "be holy as [He is] holy" (Leviticus 19:2) and that we are to be "blameless" as we live in a sinful world (Philippians 2:15). But holiness is not something we can manufacture, because we are not God. Holiness is something only God can give us out of His mercy and His love.

This is not to say that we have no responsibilities on our side. 1 John 2:3-4 tells us that if we say we love Jesus but do not obey His commands, then we are liars. James 2:14-20 says that faith without works is dead. When God mercifully saves us, our response should be grateful obedience and growing holiness over the span of our lives. We will be holy as God is holy—not because *we* are so good, but because God is so gracious.

Proverbs 24:16 tells us that "a righteous man may fall seven times, and rise again." The coin here has two sides: first, even the righteous man stumbles and falls; second, by God's grace, he gets up every time. Perfectionism is the false idea that a righteous man never falls—or when he does, he certainly doesn't admit it, lest he discourage everyone who is watching him run! When we sin and fall short of God's glorious holiness, we have no right to despair or hide, but only to confess, ask forgiveness, and get up again with God's help.

I think as wives and mothers, we have a tendency to fall into the trap of perfectionism rather easily. It starts with a very good and noble desire to set a godly example for our families, our fellow Christians, and the lost. But, before we know it, we start comparing ourselves to others and feeling we fall woefully short. That trim, beautiful newlywed in the pew in front of us always seems to have every hair in place and her clothes neat and well-pressed. We look down at the spit-up stain on our shoulder, the strained skirt seam where the toddler has been clinging, and the shoes with scuffed toes.

We look at the competent mother of six across the aisle, her perfectly obedient children sitting straight and tall in a row, her husband with his arm around her shoulders. We lean forward to catch a glimpse of our husband at the opposite end of the pew, manfully trying to subdue the antics of a three-year-old who needs to go potty...again. Deep inside, we wonder why other women seem to have it so easy.

When we compare ourselves to others this way, quite simply put, we are being fools. We judge the external, because we cannot see the heart, and we are not wise, because we do just what Paul tells us not to: compare ourselves with others (2 Corinthians 10:12, 17). We don't see the newlywed fuming on the way to church because her husband forgot something and had to go back home, making them late. We don't see the competent mother of six struggling to get a whiny toddler and grumpy teenager ready for church while searching frantically for matching shoes for herself. Because we see beautiful window dressing or catch people at their best and brightest, we assume no one is as sinful or hopelessly incapable as we often feel. Or, if they are, they certainly don't mess up as often as we seem to do.

This is folly! Ladies, we've got to get back to some pretty basic facts here: *all* people sin; *all* fall short of God's glory (Romans 3:23). There is no one who is righteous apart from Christ, and even the saintliest Christians stumble. Unfortunately, in our era of the celebrity, pop culture assaults us from every side with images of unattainable perfection. Even Christian magazines and "self-help" books often provide unbiblical, contradictory standards, adding confusion and frustration to the whole mess.

> *Pictures of perfection...make me sick*
> *and wicked. —Jane Austen*[20]

From the air-brushed models in the catalogs and the super-skinny celebrity mamas on the magazine covers to the ads for Botox™ and acid peels, we are bombarded by "perfection" on a daily basis. Feel depressed and unable to compete? Well, now you've got drugs like Zoloft™ and Prozac™. Worried about aging and getting grey hairs? You're covered there, too, as hundreds of anti-aging products beckon from the shelves, promising to smooth away wrinkles and present a "new you" almost overnight.

The truth is that however "perfect" these cultural standards may be, they do not measure up to the One Who created us in His image. The True Standard is even higher than we imagine, friends! And here's where we get to the root of perfectionism: Satan's lie to Eve in the Garden of Eden "that you will be like God" (Genesis 3:5). At its heart, perfectionism is sinful pride. We want others to think well of us, to admire us, and to desire to follow our example.

There is nothing wrong with desiring a good reputation, but not at the expense of humility and transparency. No one is perfect, save God. *No one.* Not you, not I, not the angelic-looking lady in the pew ahead of us. We need to let go of the strange notion that the only way to be a good Christian is to project an image of sinless perfection and hide our struggles and shortcomings. And so we come to the incredible paradox of the Gospel that we'll touch on many times in this book: "My grace is sufficient for thee: for my strength is made perfect in weakness. Most gladly therefore will I rather glory in my infirmities, that the power of Christ may rest upon me" (2 Corinthians 12:9). Weakness is strength? We glory in infirmity? Yes, indeed! And this beautiful paradox is what should motivate and encourage us as we serve Christ.

At its heart, perfectionism is all about pretense. It's like a grown-up version of playing dress-up. I remember putting tiny feet into Mom's church shoes, pulling a skirt up to my armpits so I wouldn't step on it, and placing one of my grandmother's hats on my head. In the mirror, I saw maturity and grace. Looking at old family photos, I just giggle at the funny jumble of mismatched clothes. Perfectionism is the crazy idea that putting on the right outfit or the fake smile will convince others that we are mature and graceful and have it all together. And it might work…for a while. But who wants to play that game full-time? Frankly, I'd be exhausted. What's more, if we kept up the charade we'd trade some very important things for the sake of our image—things like deep fellowship, godly encouragement, humble rebuke, and tenderhearted forgiveness.

Yet we do need to be careful here not to fall off the other side of the horse. God *does* call us to excel in the role He has graciously given us and strive to "adorn the gospel" as we live out God's commands (Titus 2:10). We do this by putting our best efforts into everything we do. Even the smallest tasks are filled with meaning when we approach them with godly zest and a desire to reflect (however imperfectly) the glories of the God Who gave us breathtaking mountain peaks, luxurious flowers in all colors and sizes, velvety meadows, and sweet babies made in His image. God's overflowing creativity abounds all around us, and it is honoring to Him when we seek to emulate it in our daily lives.

There are so many ways we can strive for excellence as keepers of the home without falling into the trap of perfectionism. We need to keep foremost in our minds the fact that, as people made in God's image, we must glorify Him—it's not about us.

I like to turn directly to Scripture for my inspiration here.

For starters, the Proverbs 31 woman doesn't slouch around in frumpy clothes or leave her children to fend for themselves when it comes to dressing; she makes herself beautiful clothing of "silk and purple" (Proverbs 31:22), and "all her household is clothed with scarlet" (31:21). The happy bride of the Song of Solomon rejoices to array herself for her husband with delights that include sweet perfume (Song of Solomon 4:16, 5:5), beautiful hair (6:5), and even scarlet lips that open in "comely speech" (4:3).

Both of these women deck their homes with lovely things, knowing that they bring joy to others and create an atmosphere of rest and well-being. We're not talking about home decorating on steroids here—just about the wonderful opportunity we have to reflect our Creator's eye for beauty in everything we touch. What a great privilege and honor!

So avoiding perfectionism doesn't mean embracing our inner slob. It simply means acknowledging that we are limited human beings who rely on the grace of God. And we want others to see that His grace has real transforming power. Scripture reminds us that holiness is beautiful and that Christians should reflect that beauty (Genesis 12:11; Exodus 34:29; 1 Samuel 25:3; 1 Chronicles 16:29; 2 Chronicles 20:21; Esther 2:7; Psalm 29:2; Proverbs 15:13; Song of Solomon 6:4; Ezekiel 16:11-13).

Again, let's strive for biblical balance. We'll all have "off days" at times, but we need to keep in mind that we represent not only our husbands (bringing them either honor or dishonor), but we represent Christ wherever we go. When we keep Him as our focus, we will find joy in all the things we do to glorify Him. And what a pleasure to see Christ's beauty and love reflected in the faces of fellow Christians! It's a beauty that grows from within and colors everything we do and say. It's a lasting beauty that cannot fade in spite of our human failings and imperfections (1 Peter 3:4).

Let's Get Real

You know how we can encourage each other best? It's not by playing the role of Have-It-All Hannah or Do-It-All Doris. It's by loving others enough to meet them where they are while being what *we* are: fellow sinners in need. We've got to take our eyes off the impossible, ridiculous standards of our materialistic culture with its Me-First emphasis and root ourselves firmly in the Scriptures.

We need to remember that only God is perfect, and we are not God (though Satan would like to convince us we are). And, finally, we need to understand that God is sanctifying us over time, even through our sinful mistakes, and He has promised to finish what He has begun in us (Philippians 1:6). God's grace doesn't give us license to sin, but it very definitely frees us from the bondage of perfectionism and its twin sister, pride.

Instead of worrying what others think about us, we need to care about what God thinks of us, measuring ourselves by the unchanging standard of God's Word rather than comparing ourselves to others. Instead of looking to modern-day "experts" for answers, we need to return to the "old paths" of Scripture, where there is "rest for our souls" (Jeremiah 6:16). Instead of seeking to make a name for ourselves or be "important," we need to thankfully embrace the fact that God works through humble people, small steps, and what the world considers insignificant and often thankless work.

And, for goodness' sake, we need to admit our failures! I am not a perfect wife or mother and have no delusions that I ever will be. I have no right to doubt God or lose heart when I fail in my God-given role as a wife, mother, or sister in Christ. The problem isn't that God's goals are too high or that we are too weak to reach them. There's that Gospel paradox at work again! God's strength "is made perfect in weakness" (2 Corinthians 12:9). We should not despair when we make mistakes.

My husband is a wonderful source of sanity when I lose perspective in this area. There are times he has found me running around like a chicken with its head off, trying to accomplish things *I* think are important. These are the times when he takes me gently by the shoulders, looks me in the eye, and says, "Honey, whose schedule are you living by? Who is giving you all these goals?" I sheepishly have to admit that I am the one driving myself. I've not actively sought his counsel but have just run on ahead, piling on the goals and lists and must-do activities.

When these "reality checks" come, I am always reminded that God has created me to be my *husband's* helper—not a slave to my own whims or wishes. So often we women drive ourselves harder than any taskmaster ever could, failing to submit our goals and plans to the oversight of our loving husbands. When we make it a point to ask our husbands for their priorities and structure our activities accordingly, we find rest instead of rush. I am often surprised to find that priorities I thought my husband would rate high on his list are ones he actually considers minor. This is most often a very pleasant surprise!

Many times Matt has reminded me that he would rather see me sitting on the couch, reading aloud to my children while the floor is covered with toys and books than see me stressing out over last-minute tasks that really aren't going to break our household in the long run. My husband knows I am not going to let the house go to ruin, but he also knows my tendency to let some "to-dos" become tyrannical in my own mind! I am always relieved to have him sit down and reevaluate lists and schedules and show me what I need to trim down or just stop worrying over. Your husband will be able to help you find balance here, too. Yes, we want to have clean, well-ordered households, but not at the expense of our relationships with our children or due to our vanity! When we feel weary or frazzled, it is time to stop and go to our loving head and seek his insight and direction. Just as Christ calls the weary and heavy-laden to rest, our husbands can also lead us to green pastures when we're out trying to climb mountains.

How many times has the Lord had to teach me this lesson? More than I can count. Do I despair of getting things right or simply give up and try to forge ahead in spite of weariness and frustration? I am an imperfect wife and mother, but, thanks be to God, He does not give up on me. My husband knows he is married to a flawed "ruby," but he patiently leads me time and again, showing me a picture of Christ-like love as he lifts burdens and reminds me not to pick up new ones!

We may wonder why God doesn't just give us the ability to obey perfectly and train the next generation without repeating our own childish mistakes. But this is the whole point: God gets all the glory when weak and frail sinners succeed. The Scriptures give us practical steps for discipline and training, but we cannot leave *grace* out of the equation. God works through humble sinners. *Yes*, we must be faithful to do what God says. *No*, it does not all depend on us. God is faithful.

Let's be honest: we aren't going to get it all done anyway, even if we live to be 100 and grow saintlier by the hour. Christendom isn't built in a day any more than a Christian is sanctified instantly when he is saved. This is why Christ compared His kingdom to things like mustard seeds and yeast. From tiny, humble beginnings great things grow—but only over time and through multi-generational faithfulness to God and His Word.

We aren't responsible for how all of human history turns out—only for the part God has called us to play during our own lifetime. If we get discouraged or feel overwhelmed by all there is to do, it is time to refocus and realize that God really means it when He says that His burden is light and His yoke easy (Matthew 11:30). I don't have to do it all! My children don't have to do it all! We have only to be faithful to serve God in the place He puts us and in the calling He gives us—to obey His Word; to love Him with all our heart, mind, soul, and strength, and to faithfully train our children to do the same. It gets complicated only when we clutter our expectations with worldly demands and priorities.

Let's Be Humble

Rejecting perfectionism also helps us to extend grace to others, knowing that just as we haven't "arrived," neither has anyone else. There is no excuse for looking down on others when we know how far we have to go ourselves. Because of this, we can be kind to those with whom we disagree, breaking hard bones with a gentle tongue and long forbearance (Proverbs 25:15). After all, we'd like for others to deal gently with us when they think we don't measure up, either.

None of us is immune to the disease of perfectionism. All of us want to do well. All of us want to contribute something great to the world. What Christian mother doesn't want to bring up thoughtful, godly children? But however noble our goals may be, they are utter folly if we do not keep foremost the greatest goal of them all: "He must increase; I must decrease" (John 3:30). It isn't about me. It doesn't all depend on me. I will never be "good enough," but God will always be gracious enough. His mighty strength and glorious mercy is made perfect when I am weak—*imperfect*.

I've learned (often the hard way) that it is far more important to be transparent and teachable than it is to succeed the first time or be the best at everything. When we fail, we simply demonstrate (yet again) that we are not God. We also open ourselves up to help from others. Perfectionism can trap us in a prison of our own making. If we never do anything wrong, then who has the opportunity to bless us? Serving and helping blesses the giver, not just the recipient.

I remember resting in bed after the birth of my fourth child, thinking about all the housework that wasn't getting done. "I bet the bathrooms are filthy," I mused, knowing how neat and tidy little boys are...not! I battled a desire to get up and go do something, but I knew I needed to stay put. The next morning, I heard two cheerful voices in my hall bathroom, then the sound of running water and scrubbing. My sweet husband had called a couple of young ladies we knew and asked if they would come and clean the bathrooms and straighten the house for me.

Not only did they immediately come over, but they sang and laughed while they worked, blessing me as I lay there with tears in my eyes. Here was the Body of Christ, scrubbing around my potties and taking the hair out of my drains. Whoa—that is love! But had I insisted on doing everything for myself (the perfectionist's way), I would have missed the blessing, and they would not have had the opportunity to see me at my weakest and extend love to me. I've never forgotten their happy faces or their willingness to do the dirty work.

You see, when we thank God for our weaknesses and humbly submit to correction or gratefully receive help, we open ourselves up to deep joy and contentment. We learn to stop pretending that we rely on ourselves. God will get the greater glory when others see Jesus in you in spite of your weaknesses— or may I say *because* of your weaknesses.

In 1 Corinthians 1:27 Paul writes, "But God hath chosen the foolish things of the world to confound the wise; and God hath chosen the weak things of the world to confound the things which are mighty." Then in 2 Corinthians 12:9-11, he observes:

> *And he said unto me, "My grace is sufficient for thee: for my strength is made perfect in weakness." Most gladly therefore will I rather glory in my infirmities, that the power of Christ*

may rest upon me. Therefore I take pleasure in infirmities, in reproaches, in necessities, in persecutions, in distresses for Christ's sake: for when I am weak, then am I strong.

Read it again, sisters! When you are weak, let out a whoop, because whatever you are able to do comes through the grace of God. When you are nothing, shout "Hallelujah!" because Jesus is getting all the glory and honor for what you accomplish. God loves His weak, imperfect, needy people. He didn't choose us because we won some international awards for strength, beauty, or intelligence. He has made us for Himself, and He is going to provide us with everything we need to serve Him and love others through our imperfect homes and families. What a joy to serve our perfect Creator, Who made us in His image and is transforming us (slowly, but surely) into the image of His perfect Son.

Chapter Six

Mamas, Don't Let Your Babies Grow Up to Be Housewives

Jennie Chancey

"You won't catch *me* being Little Suzy Homemaker!" the teenager scoffed. The young women in line in front of me burst into laughter. While waiting at the grocery store, I had been privy to a loud conversation among three college students, all gossiping about their boyfriends. The first speaker had just "dumped" her steady when he expressed an interest in settling down and starting a family after college. One of her friends rolled her eyes in disbelief. "No way!" she exclaimed. "I won't even *think* about a family until I've had time to do my own thing for a while." The others nodded in agreement.

Just a month later, I picked up a copy of a news story claming that nearly 80% of young women in Ivy League schools plan to quit work or scale way back on time at a job when they marry and have children—they want to be homemakers.[21] The story created a fury, as feminists vehemently denied the statistics, while many brave young women chimed in to agree that babies need to be raised by their own mommies.

It seems clear that we live in confused times. Girls receive mixed messages on every side. Even when small glimmers of hope appear, the other side rushes to deny and deride. Their message is loud and clear: marriage is a last resort; bringing up your own children is a waste of time and talent; and if anything stands between you and your goals in life, you should just sweep it (or him?) aside.

Even in Christian churches, homemaking and motherhood have fallen from favor. Teachers encourage young girls to do their own thing and get the "most" they can out of life before getting married and starting a family.

Many even take Scripture out of context to justify delaying or foregoing marriage, pointing to passages like 1 Corinthians 7:8 for support. For the record, when St. Paul declared that he wished the unmarried would remain single, he was careful to state that this was "not a commandment" (7:7) and that some would have a special gift of celibacy—but not all, since "every man hath his proper gift of God" (7:7). Paul's suggestion that single men and women in Corinth remain unmarried was due to "the present distress" (7:26) in Achaia at the time of his writing—an apparent season of persecution that the Corinthian church found themselves embroiled in which "rendered the cares of the marriage life undesirable."[22] As commentator Albert Barnes explains, "[Paul] by no means meant that this should be a permanent arrangement."[23] That Paul's counsel was limited to the Corinthians' "distress" (and, by implication, similar difficulties other singles might face thereafter) is made clear by reading his letter to Timothy where he affirmed the exact opposite:

> *I will therefore that the younger women marry, bear children, guide the house, give none occasion to the adversary to speak reproachfully.* (1 Timothy 5:14)

Even if a young woman desires to marry, there are counselors quick to step in and encourage her not to "tie herself down" to the home. Pastors neatly sweep Titus 2 and 1 Peter 3 under the rug, assuring us that all those passages were purely cultural and don't apply in our modern times. Christian teachers urge daughters to follow the career track so they won't "waste" their God-given talents, making homemaking and child-training sound like a last resort or a backwater for women with few talents.

A terrible irony in all of this is that we Christians are limping about twenty years behind the world, which means we are set to repeat the same worldly mistakes instead of pointing the way out of the incredible mess that has been created by daycare, government schooling, behavioral drugs, and, at the bottom of it all, absent parents. Dozens of secular and religious writers have published books documenting the deplorable state of American children—children who need their own mommies and daddies caring for them at home, not just another institutional solution or government program.[24]

Why are Christians following the rest of the lemmings over the cliff? I believe the answer is two-fold. First, we have traded the clear teachings of the Bible for "hip" and "relevant" platitudes that affirm worldliness instead of confronting it.

Secondly, we have a narrow idea of what it means to be a keeper at home. Let's start with the second issue, because it will lead us right back around to the chief problem.

Big Houses, Empty Yards, and Lonely Neighbors

We live in a materialistic nation kept afloat by consumerism. We are encouraged to window shop in our magazines, buy things we don't need, and covet things we cannot afford. Personal debt is at an all-time high as people spend far more than they earn to keep themselves entertained and well fed. "McMansions" go up at an astonishing rate, particularly when you consider that people are having fewer children and do not need all the space. The security industry is booming as people seek to protect possessions they are rarely home to enjoy.[25] The service industry (dry cleaning, fast food, maids, etc.) grows every year.[26] Homemakers? Who needs 'em?

Because of the gimme-gimme culture we live in, we've lost our understanding of the meaning of home and homemaking. The professional catalogs and home decorating magazines don't help much, either. There's no sin apparent in all those beautiful pictures of just-so houses with perfectly matched furniture and coordinated color schemes. Let's face it. For most of us, fingerprints, juice spills, and well-used bathrooms are part of our overall "décor!" And you know what? That's life!

It doesn't help that our culture now glorifies the "have-it-all" woman: you know, the one with the ultra-slim figure, power suit, perfect hair, successful career, beautiful home, and, on top of it all, the adoring husband and two perfect children. Problem is, that woman doesn't really exist. She's a figment of our feminist imagination—nothing more than wishful thinking by a generation of women who have pursued the superwoman myth and found themselves on an endless treadmill of 9-5 jobs, hurried housework, numberless kids' activities, and exhausting "entertainment."

There just isn't a way to have it all. Yet our culture insists that *this* is the successful woman. To settle for less would mean stifling your talents and gifts, or, worse, shriveling up into a pathetic nobody who never gets any glory. No wonder girls are taught to look everywhere *but* home for fulfillment, satisfaction, and long-term happiness. Homemaker? Not I.

What's Our Excuse?

Do you ever think about our foremothers—you know, all those quaint ladies who eked a bare existence out of the wilderness, saw numbers of their own children die, lost husbands in far-off battles, then picked up the pieces and moved on? We don't have "superwomen" today—no matter what the magazines say or the movies seek to project. Our ancestors were the *real* wonder women. Would we still praise God if we had to keep dirt floors clean, children healthy, and gardens growing in a strange new environment far from family and friends?

I have many books about the men, women, and families who settled America. I've marveled at their pluck, their determination, and their willingness to face death in order to provide something better for their children and grandchildren. And I am always humbled by what I read, because I realize that I am a big wimp who doesn't have a thing to complain about. Just read this passage from the book, *Woman's Life in*

Colonial Days, by Carl Holliday, published in 1922:

> There is a decided tendency among modern housewives to take a hostile view of the ever recurring task of preparing food for the family; but if these housewives were compelled suddenly to revert to the method and amount of cooking of colonial days, there would be universal rebellion...
>
> We must remember...that the greater part of all food consumed in a family was prepared through its every stage by that family. No factory-canned goods, no ready-to-warm soups, no evaporated fruits, no potted meats stood upon the grocers' shelves as a very present help in time of need. On the farm or plantation and even in the smaller towns the meat was raised, slaughtered, and cured at home, the wheat, oats, and corn grown, threshed and frequently made into flour and meal by the family, the fruit dried or preserved by the housewife...
>
> And yet with such cumbersome utensils, the good wives of all the colonies prepared meals that would drive the modern cook to distraction...To be a housewife in colonial days evidently required the strength of Hercules, the skill of Tubal Cain, and the patience of Job.[27]

So what's our excuse? We complain that it takes so much time to prepare meals, yet we have freezers, food processors, electric beaters, and stoves with instant heat (no flint or borrowed coals required). We sigh over the mounds of laundry that never seem to end, yet we don't have to boil a cauldron of water, scald our hands to scrub the clothes, then squeeze out the excess liquid by hand before hanging everything to dry. We don't have to heat heavy irons on a hot stove or make homemade starch for shirts and collars, either.

Oh, and don't forget that the colonial women who did this were hospitable women, constantly welcoming people into their homes and making meals stretch to fit them all. There was no yearly vacation at the beach or long weekends of just sitting around, watching the tube.

I am certainly not saying that our foremothers were perfect women who had it all together and never complained. They did their share of worrying and stumbling. But they did not have the luxury to dwell upon their shortcomings or fret about how they measured up to everyone else. There just was not the time, and the whole notion of self-pity was roundly condemned by the mothers who trained up the generation of women who would settle the West, often facing long stretches of lonely prairie without a near neighbor.

My great-great-great-grandmother, Mary Ethell, was one of those women. Her husband was a circuit-riding preacher who left their Oklahoma farm for weeks at a time to take God's Word to far-flung settlements. Mary could have become bitter toward her husband or resentful about all the work, but she just rolled up her sleeves and got busy. Chickens weren't going to deliver eggs to the door, and corn wasn't going to shuck itself.

"Well," you say, "that's just the point, though. We have all these modern conveniences now so that we don't have to do the things our ancestors did. We really don't need 'housewives' anymore, because *anyone* can run a dishwasher or vacuum." Doesn't this just beg the question? Someone *does* have to do the work. It isn't going to do itself.[28] Sure, "anyone" could do it, but God has providentially given it to *me* to do—and it is my job to see that it's done right and to train my children to work alongside me.

Not only that, but God has shown us through the models of Proverbs 31 and Titus 2 that older women and younger women can help one another in making a home a vibrant center of creativity and shared work—not a prison of drudgery. Those maidens of Proverbs 31 learned the detailed management of a productive home from the accomplished keeper of that home—right under her watchful eye. There is a wonderful reciprocity here.

I've been very blessed to have parents send daughters to stay with me after the birth of four of my children. Some stayed a few days; others stayed for weeks. My mother and mother-in-law have also come to make sure I kept off my feet. I cannot stress enough how incredibly beneficial it has been to have this help, and I have profusely thanked the families who have sent daughters to be my hands and feet so that I could get the extra rest I needed. In generations past, women could take such help for granted; we cannot do that today. It is a rare gift.

I think this is one area we need to reclaim for our daughters and granddaughters. I truly believe that *this* is the spirit of Titus 2. Homemaking isn't about doing it all—*all by ourselves*. It is about a beautiful principle that we find throughout Scripture: "My life for yours." As these young women have blessed me, I have been able to encourage them and teach them, too. As these older women have reached out to me, they've given me jewels of wisdom from their years of experience. It's not "cheating" to seek help or to give it to those who need it; it's just the simple "do unto others" of Christ.

At its heart, all Christian service is about humility and transparency—about confessing our faults to each other and extending grace. Unfortunately, the modern church has so disconnected itself from biblical reality that we have embraced a radical individualism that divorces us from one another and cripples the church. The loss of the Christian homemaker is a devastating one—and all the more so because we do not understand what we have lost, nor do we appreciate what it takes to establish a godly, hospitable home.

You see, homemaking is far more than housekeeping. We need to toss out narrow modern-day conceptions that are built around stereotypes and restore our vision based upon God's Word. When we do, we can begin to understand why the biblical family is an indispensable foundation stone of a healthy society—and what happens when that stone is removed.

You want to watch a culture self-destruct? Eliminate the fathers, make the mothers neglect their children, and teach everyone to forsake the weak, the needy, and the elderly. It has happened before. Just read your history. The Spartans declared that children were the property of the State, better trained by experts than by their own parents.[29] The ancient Romans exposed unwanted babies and the elderly, leaving them to die in isolation.[30] Euthanasia and abortion are not new, nor are the less distasteful sins of family disintegration and the welfare state.

These things are happening in our nation now, just as they have happened in the past when men and nations rejected God's ways. Man without Christ is lost. Families who reject the clear biblical commands for fathers, mothers, husbands, wives, and children are doomed to follow the same downward spiral, no matter how "relevant" their counselors tell them they are being.

God's Word raises a standard His people can confidently trust. This is why ancient Israel had strong laws to protect widows, orphans, and strangers. It is why Christians went against cultural trends in pagan Rome, rescuing babies and the unwanted from exposure and certain death.[31] It's why they boldly took care of plague victims when pagan doctors fled, causing heathen kings to note their genuine hospitality and fearlessness.[32] Vibrant Christian homes where families work together, contented in God's wise division of labor, can quite literally change the world.

How Hard Can It Be?

Betty Friedan's[33] old saw that anyone can manage a home and that it doesn't take brains to bring up children just doesn't jive with reality. Many women who return home have a rude awakening when they realize it is a life-changing and challenging calling. But when they look around for instruction or inspiration, they find that the older women are often out pursuing their own ends. Today it is like finding an oasis in the desert to discover a competent homemaker who is capable and willing to teach a young gal the ropes.

I *was* raised by a Proverbs 31 woman who taught me how to cook, clean, organize, sew, upholster, paint, decorate...the list goes on! I can imagine how difficult it would be to manage eight children and a very busy household if I had not been trained to do it from the ground up. Yet I know women who succeed and thrive in spite of a lack of training; they roll up their sleeves and learn as they go. They are doing it despite the widespread shelving of Titus 2, and they are determined that their own daughters won't have to struggle alone as they did.

Have you had the privilege of visiting a family whose home is a busy hive of service, productivity, love, laughter, and hospitality? Such homes are a balm, holding out refreshment and encouragement without pretension. Such families are rare, because so few women truly embrace their God-given role as wise guardians and keepers of the home. Yes, *guardians*. The Greek word for "keeper at home" (*oikourgos*) is literally translated "the watch, or keeper."[34] Home is too important to be left to itself; it is something precious to be tended, cared for, kept, and, yes, guarded. God has given women a sphere that is naturally and wonderfully their own to manage and wisely govern.

The home is a tiny world—a cosmos all to itself. Do you want to rule the world? God has given you the universe of your home to manage. Your job is to make this small kingdom a picture of God's greater kingdom—a kingdom in which the subjects are in order and obey their king; a kingdom where beauty shines in every word and deed; a kingdom that welcomes friends and strangers with abundant hospitality and gracious care. Many writers today chronicle the "death of the West"— meaning Western culture. Look around at the homes that make up our culture. There is the root of the problem. Homes that are emptied of their meaning and purpose make up the culture in which we live. When homes do not have creative, happy, intelligent mothers keeping them, their occupants go elsewhere to learn how to behave, to learn what music to love, to learn what art to imitate. Are you building culture in your home? Are you training your children to be the image-bearers of God in this world? This is your calling.

The dominion mandate of Genesis was given to *both* Adam and Eve. Both were called to be fruitful, to fill the earth and subdue it. King Adam was not complete without Queen Eve. The dominion mandate isn't just for the "out there, somewhere" of the workaday world; it is for the "in here, right here" of the productive Christian home. There again we see the beauty of God's created order, which needs both Adam's calling and Eve's calling *together* to accomplish the fullness of the kingdom.

You see, homemaking isn't about the house itself or the things it contains. Being keepers at home is about focusing upon the Lord in all the everydayness so that our houses become centers of hospitality, forgiveness, training, business, welfare, charity, shared mourning and celebration, and—oh, yes—lots of tracked-in mud, crumbs under the chairs, and everything else that goes with human beings. We must not lose sight of the fact that our homes are God-given tools to bless others. They aren't the end goal; they are, simply, one of the *means* to the end. And what is the end? Dying to self, laying down our lives, serving others that Christ may grow His kingdom and transform the world and ourselves as we do things His way.

Seek the old paths and walk ye in them, for there you shall find rest for your souls. (Jeremiah 6:16)

When we find ourselves bogged down in a cultural quagmire, the answer is to *go back*. We must do as the Bereans did, searching the Scriptures to see what is true and what we must do (Acts 17:11). The answer is most assuredly *not* to consult modern-day "experts" who attempt to rewrite the Scriptures to suit our personal lifestyles and wishes.

This is the simple crux of the matter: modern anti-homemaking teachers do not urge their readers to believe and trust in the simple, plain teachings found in Scripture regarding husbands and wives, fathers and mothers, parents and children. The secular feminists toss the Word out completely as absurd and irrelevant. The "evangelical" feminists toss out four thousand years of Church history and declare that egalitarianism has been God's intent all along—patriarchy was just a temporary evil.[35]

What is tragic is that both views embrace relativism—the belief that what is "right for you" may not be "right for me," and that's okay. You believe God's Word calls women to be keepers at home? Fine and dandy. If that's how you find fulfillment, go for it. But if I believe God wants me to reach my full potential in a career outside the family, that's fine for me, and you can't to appeal to Proverbs 31, Titus 2, or 1 Peter 3, all of which were the products of a backwards culture.

But biblical reality is far richer, and God is not limited by the cultures and people He has to work with down through the ages. He *designed* the culture He desires us to pass down to the coming generations. After bringing the Israelites out of Egypt, God declared that all *other* cultures were "backwards," but He was going to create one that modeled His kingdom to the world. When other nations looked at Israel obeying God's perfect law, they would marvel:

Therefore be careful to observe them; for this is your wisdom and your understanding in the sight of the peoples who will hear all these statutes and say, "Surely this great nation is a wise and understanding people." For what great nation is there that has God so near to it, as the Lord our God is to us, for whatever reason we may call upon Him? And what great nation is there that has such statutes and righteous judgments as are in all this law which I set before you this day? (Deuteronomy 4:7-8)

When Israel kept God's commandments, they would be abundantly blessed and protected, but when they disobeyed, they would become just like the pagan cultures around them, forced to eat the woeful fruits of their rebellion (see Deuteronomy 28). Before Moses died, he sang the praises of God's perfect commands for His people as he warned them not to reject them:

Hearken, ye heavens, and I will speak; and let the earth hear the words of my mouth. My doctrine shall drop as the rain, and my speech shall still as the dew, as the shower upon the herbs, and as the great rain upon the grass. Perfect is the work of the mighty God; for all His ways are judgment. God is true and without wickedness. Just and righteous is He. (Deuteronomy 32:1-4)

Earlier, God made it clear that He was setting His people apart from the pagan nations and cultures around them, making a clean break from their practices:

And the Lord spake unto Moses, saying, "Speak unto the

> *children of Israel, and say unto them, I am the Lord your God. After the doings of the land of Egypt, wherein ye dwelt, shall ye not do; and after the manner of the land of Canaan, whither I will bring you, shall ye not do, neither walk in their ordinances. But do after my judgments, and keep mine ordinances, to walk therein: I am the Lord your God."* (Leviticus 18:1-4)

When we look around at a culture that is reviving and embracing pagan beliefs and practices, I don't see a cause for rejoicing. I see cause for repentance and a firmer determination to obey God's Word in spite of cultural pressures to the contrary. Christian homemaking is outdated and replaceable? Says who? And where is the biblical assertion that God's model needs revising and updating to fit the times rather than the reverse—that the times need to be brought into greater conformity to God's perfect, timeless Word?

So How Do We Do This?

I'll grant you that the Gospel makes little sense to the human mind. Christ didn't come to be served. He didn't come to demand recognition. He came to be the least and last and to lay down His life for His sheep. You want to be equal with God? Die—it's that simple. Why is God's role for women so important? Because God says when we reject it, we blaspheme His Word (Titus 2:5). That means we essentially tell the world that God doesn't really mean what He says and doesn't know what He is doing. "We've got a better way to save the world, Lord," we say. "See, we're going to create experts to bring up our children, and we'll let secretaries help our husbands. We'll hand hospitality over to restaurants and hotels. It will be so much more efficient than this outdated institution of the family!"

Here is where we must recover biblical sanity. At its heart, homemaking is about accepting God's Word and laying down our lives for the brethren. It is about keeping our eyes firmly fixed upon Christ, Who calls us to serve Him in the seemingly insignificant tasks of everyday living, training the next generation, reaching out to the needy, demonstrating hospitality to saints and strangers, and living for Christ's "well done" rather than for the praise and recognition of others.

And *that's* the secret to a happy and blessed life. Die to live. Go last to be first. Give to receive. Make yourself least to be greatest. Homemakers? *God created women to fulfill this unique role.* That's all we need to know to rest in our callings. We can trust Him to conquer the world, one heart at a time, as we live sacrificially and rejoice in His narrow way.

Chapter Seven

The Search for a "Stepford" Husband

Jennie Chancey

Pop culture today glorifies effeminacy in men. From television shows like *Queer Eye for the Straight Guy* and the glorification of "metrosexuals"[36] who are in touch with their feminine side, to fumbling, emotionally immature sitcom dads, the message is clear: maleness is something we have to "fix," and all those old masculine role models just won't do.

One of the strange ironies of feminism is that it isn't feminine. For several generations, women have been told they have to be more like men, adopting male occupations, mannerisms, and clothing. The "hook-up"[37] culture even encourages women to be as promiscuous as the proverbial bad boys, urging them to go on the prowl and to forget about emotional and spiritual intimacy—as if lowering the bar for everyone will somehow raise us to true equality.

While women have pursued masculine traits, men have faced pressure to soften their maleness and adopt feminine traits. In the meantime, a generation of boys finds itself on

Ritalin in an attempt to suppress masculine energy before it even has a chance to express itself, making war on boyhood.[38]

What is going on with all this push toward androgyny? Are we really supposed to believe that utopia is just around the corner if men will simply make themselves more like women and women more like men? Where do we find answers in these postmodern times?

Asking the One Who Made Them Male and Female

And the LORD God said, "It is not good that the man should be alone; I will make him an help meet for him." (Genesis 2:18)

When God finished each day of creation, He pronounced it "good." The first time God declared a part of His creation "not good" was when Adam stood alone in the Garden of Eden. As God brought the animals to Adam to name, Adam saw a pattern: male and female. Each animal had its counterpart. Yet Adam was incomplete. God had not yet created any other person to complete him.

Finally, God put the man to sleep and fashioned a helper suitable for him from Adam's own body. When God presented woman to man, Adam uttered the first poem: "This at last is bone of my bones and flesh of my flesh; she shall be called Woman, because she was taken out of Man" (vs. 23). The poetry here is heightened when we realize that the Hebrew words used for woman and man are "*ishah*" and "*ish*," clearly demonstrating woman's derivation from man.

There are egalitarians[39] today who insist that, rather than being a detailed version of Genesis 1 (which synopsizes the creation of man), Genesis 2 is a different story altogether. According to these teachers, Adam was originally male *and* female (Genesis 1) before being divided into separate male and female beings (Genesis 2).[40] Right off the bat, we're in murky waters. If God's Word cannot be trusted to give us the straight truth about the created order, then what's to keep us from discounting other parts of Scripture or picking and choosing what we find "rational" or "believable?"[41]

Whenever someone comes to us with a "new and improved" reading of Scripture, we need to look into the long history of the church and the testimony of faithful saints of the past to see if "new" arguments and interpretations are actually old heresies recycled.[42]

When someone tells us that God really didn't intend for us to embrace gender distinctions but to "move beyond" them to some androgynous utopia,[43] several questions should come to mind right away:

- Why did God create male and female with distinct biological traits and call them "very good" if androgyny is the ideal?

- If husbands and wives are interchangeable, then why did God give Adam his calling first, then create a helper for him?

- Why didn't God make women exactly like men in their muscle mass, bone density, and overall physical design if women are meant to fill the same roles as men and even compete with men on a level playing field?

- Why did God call Adam to account after the fall rather than calling Eve (who fell for the Serpent's lie and took the fruit first) or calling both Adam and Eve together? (Note that Paul in 1 Corinthians 15:22 squarely lays the blame for the fall at Adam's feet, not Eve's—hardly egalitarian!)

- If fathers and mothers are interchangeable, then why are human children "knit together" in the mother's womb, and why did God design the woman's breast to provide the best nourishment for a growing child?

- Related to the last question, if "mother" and "father" are indistinguishable terms, why does Scripture specifically provide the model of father-rule, such as when God says, "For I have chosen [Abraham], that he may command his children and his household after him to keep the way of the LORD by doing righteousness and justice, so that the LORD may bring to Abraham what he has promised him" (Genesis 18:19)?

- Why does Scripture give special status to widows and orphans and declare that caring for them is "pure religion… undefiled" (James 1:27)? Why not widowers? Why declare that a man who doesn't provide for the widows and orphans in his own household is an "infidel" (1 Timothy 5:8) if women can and should provide for themselves?

- If submission is so odious and culture-bound, then why did Christ model submission to the Father, reminding His disciples that, "I can of Myself do nothing. As I hear, I judge; and My judgment is righteous, because I do not seek My own will but the will of the Father who sent Me" (John 5:30) and "For I have not spoken on My own authority; but the Father who sent Me gave Me a command, what I should say and what I should speak" (John 12:49)?

Scripture emphatically does not suggest that women should be treated as chattel or children.[44] Furthermore, nowhere in Scripture is it implied that women are the "lesser" image of God—or that they're any less valuable, intelligent, or trustworthy. Scripture is unambiguous: male and female *both* bear the image of God: "So God created man in his own image, in the image of God created he him; male and female created he them" (Genesis 1:27).

But God's image is by no means androgynous; to insist that it is does violence to the perfection of His created order which shows that male and female are distinct, particular halves of a whole—humanity.

Scripture reminds us of these beautiful differences over and over again. To settle a question about divorce, Jesus pointed back to the created order: "Have ye not read, that he which made them at the beginning made them male and female, and said, 'For this cause shall a man leave father and mother, and shall cleave to his wife: and they twain shall be one flesh?'" (Matthew 19:4-5).

Paul also affirmed the created order when he wrote, "For the man is not of the woman; but the woman of the man. Neither was the man created for the woman; but the woman for the man" (1 Corinthians 11:8-9). Far from seeking to put women down, our gracious Lord lifts them up, condemning the evils of easy divorce, which allowed men to sinfully put their wives away without biblical cause. And Paul goes on to remind men that, even though woman was fashioned from and for man, yet man is born of woman and is also dependent upon her for life (1 Corinthians 11:12).

Even more wondrous is the fact that, when we live our respective roles given to us by God, we present to the world a picture of Christ and His Bride, the Church:

> *Wives, submit yourselves unto your own husbands, as unto the Lord. For the husband is the head of the wife, even as Christ is the head of the church: and he is the saviour of the body. Therefore as the church is subject unto Christ, so let the wives be to their own husbands in every thing. Husbands, love your wives, even as Christ also loved the church, and gave himself for it; That he might sanctify and cleanse it with the washing of water by the word, That he might present it to himself a glorious church, not having spot, or wrinkle, or any such thing; but that it should be holy and without blemish.* (Ephesians 5:25-27)

Our calling goes far beyond the mundane and the earthly—it reaches to Heaven, of which we are to give a picture (albeit an imperfect one) here on earth. As women, we have the very noble and awe-inspiring task of showing the world what a "glorious church" looks like as it submits to and honors its Head. We cannot do this if we are busy trying to erase our distinctives or downplay our differences. We need male. We need female. We need husbands and wives, fathers and mothers. When we accept the "very good" of creation, then we look to the rest of Scripture to show us how to live out those different, complementary roles, and we find that God hasn't left us to grope in the dark.

Finding Mr. Right—On My Terms, If You Please

Several years ago, I hosted a Bible study in my home for teenage girls. We read together and discussed many things, but some of our best conversations occurred over tea and scones served afterwards. I'll never forget one young woman telling me about her best friend, who was majoring in music in college with an emphasis on performance.

When asked if she ever planned to marry, the young musician said, "Well, I'd like to get married one day, but only if my husband plans to support me in my calling. God has given me gifts that I just have to use; I couldn't let anyone get in the way of my talents." This was before feminism had taken such a strong hold in many churches, and I was surprised at the comment. I asked the young women in my study what they thought about this sentiment and was glad to hear them immediately refer to Genesis to refute the idea that a man is called to be a woman's helper. One of them said, "I'd have no respect for a man who wanted to follow me around and say, 'Whatever you want, dear.'"

Yet I meet girls today who aren't so sure. They seem genuinely confused, as effeminacy in men and the masculinization of women have proceeded apace in the modern church, and more and more people embrace egalitarianism in pursuit of their own desires and "talents." Left to gather dust in the corner is the notion that the Lord gives women gifts and abilities that will perfectly complete and help their husbands, creating strong, kingdom-building marriages and families for the glory of God.

No talents are wasted in the Kingdom of God, and putting gifts to use in the service of husbands and godly households is *not* akin to burying talents in the ground. Proverbs 31 should put that notion firmly to rest, as Scripture demonstrates the wonderful scope for creativity, productivity, and achievement given to the godly keeper of the home.

When I was growing up, I loved to write. My father was an author and helped me to develop my writing skills, teaching me to edit and fine-tune my work. I published several articles while still a teenager and looked forward to writing for the rest of my life, trusting the Lord to use this passion as He saw fit. Little did I know that, six hundred miles away, my future mother-in-law was praying for the Lord to send her son an editor for a wife! My husband is a gifted communicator and often has opportunities to write speeches, op-ed pieces, and articles for various publications. But he hates editing and always has. I love to edit!

Ours was truly a marriage made in Heaven. The skills and talents that the Lord developed in me throughout my years of homeschooling are ones that perfectly complement my husband's particular calling. He has thanked his mother many times for praying so specifically for his future wife. And, in turn, my husband has always encouraged me to use my love of writing when it does not distract me from or compete with my God-given duties as wife and mother.

We need to remind our daughters that they aren't looking for a "made-to-order" husband who will follow all of *their* plans and dreams. Waiting for Mr. Right doesn't mean holding out until "Mr. Mom" comes along—you know, the guy who does all the dishes, sweeps, folds laundry, then babysits while his wife runs around with the girls. There absolutely is a place for husbands to bless their wives by helping with a busy household, but God has given us a division of labor for a reason; no one has to "do it all."

I don't have to go out and earn money to keep a roof over our heads *and* come home to take care of the daily housekeeping tasks. My husband shouldn't have to do double duty, either. When I am consistently and faithfully fulfilling my responsibilities, my husband is free to do the things he was created to do. There is no room for bitterness in this arrangement. This is a cause for thankfulness!

The beauty of following our biblical roles is that wives not only get to fulfill the Dominion Mandate with their husbands in different but equally important ways, but they are able to present to the world a picture of Christ's Bride, the Church, at the same time. Christ is the Head of the Church—not her slave-driver or her sugar-daddy. The Bride is joyfully joined to the Head, Who has "raised us up with Him and seated us with Him in the Heavenly places" (Ephesians 2:6). This is the beautiful paradox of the gospel: the last shall be first, and the least shall be greatest (Proverbs 25:6-7; Mark 9:35).

Submission, therefore, does not place us in a position of dishonor or shame; rather, it provides the opportunity for our head to show us greater honor by cherishing us through Christ-like leadership.[45] This in turn illustrates the incredible love of our Savior, Who "made Himself nothing" and "humbled

Himself" to die for us in spite of the fact that He is the Creator of the universe (Philippians 2:5-11).

When husbands love their wives as Christ loved the Church and gave Himself for her, they demonstrate the humble leadership of Jesus. When wives honor their husbands and "obey...without fear" (1 Peter 3:6), they demonstrate the trustful obedience of the Church to Christ's rule. There is harmony and grace in a marriage built on the Edenic order of creation—never abuse or disunity. But when we rebel against this order, we become the foolish women of Proverbs 14:1 and pull our houses down with our own hands.

The Fruits of Effeminacy

Even a brief look at the disintegrating culture around us should warn us that squashing biblical roles for men and women is a bad idea. Secular psychologists and sociologists document the deterioration of mothers and children when the father is absent.[46] The welfare state has risen on the backs of fatherless households, replacing father-rule with state-rule.[47]

Feminists who decry the deprivations of single moms and children on welfare are in a sticky situation that their worldview cannot help. If men and women are interchangeable and totally equal, then why is it any more of a problem for women to be abandoned than it is for men? Why the predominance of single moms on state aid?[48]

There's a catch-22 here noted by many welfare reformers: moms who live on welfare (state replacing the husband) can be with their children; moms who leave welfare to work cannot—and children need both parents and a stable environment to thrive.[49] So the state must step in and become father as well as husband. Rejecting the biblical model brings very real, very serious consequences.

We cannot escape the fact that men are held responsible by God for the care and welfare of their families. When men abdicate their role as providers, societal chaos results. Mothers must shift for themselves, relying on daycare to bring up their children while they put food on the table. Boys without a strong male role model often become angry and violent, lacking a productive outlet for their energies.[50]

Women do not just automatically "evolve" into a new androgyny, easily taking on the role of father as well as mother, provider as well as helper. Practically speaking, it just doesn't work, and no amount of wrestling and wrangling with Scripture will force better outcomes.

In the insistence that we don't want "Stepford" wives, we need to be careful that we don't end up creating "Stepford" husbands. Flattening maleness will not lead us into a new age of greater harmony; in fact, we know from history and Scripture that it does just the reverse.

Being a Curse or a Blessing: The Choice is Ours

For she hath cast down many wounded: yea, many strong men have been slain by her. (Proverbs 7:26)

The book of Proverbs is a gold mine of wisdom. For Christian women, Proverbs 31 immediately comes to mind, but there is far more to glean from this marvelous book. Chapter seven paints a picture of the wayward woman, whose "feet would not stay at home" (vs. 11). The second half of chapter nine contrasts the foolish woman with the beautiful personification of wisdom that is given in chapter eight and the first half of chapter nine. It is clear that we have a choice to be foolish or wise, to pattern ourselves after the biblical model of godly femininity or the sinful model of the foolish usurper.

There are so many stories in Scripture that show us the faithfulness of wise women. I think of Sarah, Naomi, Ruth, Abigail, Jael, Esther, Elizabeth, Mary, Dorcas, Lydia, and the many women who supported Jesus in his ministry. Then there are also stories of foolish women who disobeyed the Lord and serve as examples of what we do *not* want to emulate, like Lot's wife and daughters, Michal, Athaliah, Jezebel, the haughty women of Isaiah 3, Sapphira, and the bickering Euodia and Syntyche.

Isaiah 3:1-12 paints a picture of the cultural suicide that results when a nation rejects God's commands. Among the curses listed is that "children are their oppressors, and women rule over them." In the verses leading up to this, God declares that He has taken away "the mighty man and...the honorable man" from His people because of their disobedience to His law. The loss of biblical manliness is not a blessing, and women taking charge in the face of effeminacy is a judgment (just as Deborah told the cowardly men of Israel in Judges 4). Clearly, androgyny or interchangeable roles wasn't God's plan from the beginning. Do we want to be a part of a curse or part of a blessing?

God's Word is clear: when His people obey Him, marriages, families, and cultures thrive (Deuteronomy 11:8-28). Men provide for their families in spite of having to work "by the sweat of their brow," and women birth and nurture children in spite of the pain and difficulty of childbearing. (And note that work and childbearing aren't curses; it's the difficulty and pain associated with them that are. Yet God even redeems work and childbearing as He says in Ecclesiastes 9:7 and John 16:22.) Together, both parents can follow the commands of Deuteronomy 6:6-9 and Ephesians 6:4, training their children in righteousness without despair or futility.

Both parents impart God's commands to their children through their respective roles—fathers patiently leading and training, mothers instructing with wisdom and demonstrating honor to authority. Again, there is no room for selfishness or self-exaltation—for either men or women. Wives are not to be mindless doormats; God rather requires wisdom and discretion of them. Husbands must shun effeminacy and refuse to abdicate their God-given authority.

Learning to Powerfully Support and Help a Husband

So, what happens when we say "yes" to biblical manhood and "no" to effeminacy? Scripture shows us that a man who is supported and aided by his capable, submissive wife grows in honor and ability: "Her husband is known in the gates, when he sitteth among the elders of the land" (Proverbs 31:23). This is a man who is known for his wisdom and judgment. No one can point to an out-of-control household behind him and dismiss his advice. "The heart of her husband doth safely trust in her, so that he shall have no need of spoil" (Proverbs 31:11). Because this wife manages her household so well, her husband does not have to micro-manage. He trusts her judgment. He relies on her skills and doesn't have to bear a double burden.

Stacy and I have sought the opinions of hundreds of real-life wives and mothers on the importance of affirming the husband's leadership and provision for the family. We have marked one thread that ties all of these ladies of varying backgrounds and situations together: honor. All of these women have noted the very real benefits and blessings that come as they honor their husbands so that they may grow in their God-given role, succeed as providers, and "safely trust" in their wives.

What these ladies are doing is very down-to-earth and often extremely simple. These wives recognize that they are sinful women married to sinful men, but all of them have learned how to show respect and honor—and see the Lord work through their very human, very ordinary husbands. Besides making sure their husbands don't have to worry about the home front (or come home to act as disaster relief), these wives make it a point to build up their spouses as brothers in Christ:

> I make a real effort to always speak well of my husband. Even when he does things that turn out to not have been wise, or that have made me very unhappy, I do my best to be supportive and positive when talking to others—and him! By me being careful in what I say, and not speaking ill of my husband, he doesn't have to worry about people having a poor opinion of him. He is well thought of in our community, and while that is in large part because he is a compassionate, generous person, I believe it is also because of the effort I make show him love and respect, no matter what. —Tracy D.

I praise him in front of his face and behind his back. He does not think highly enough of himself, and I try to make sure he knows how wonderful I think he is! I am blessed to have such an outstanding husband. —Evelyn M.

I never speak ill of him to others. He says, "Even when I deserve it, my wife never puts me in an ill light to friends and acquaintances. She speaks nothing but praises, and I find that this attitude then transcends to other practical matters. I know that, no matter what, she will only do that which is best for me and our family." —Laura L.

One of the most foolish things a woman can do to her husband is to emasculate him by putting him down publicly. Complaining about his bad habits or revealing his weaknesses is not only foolhardy, it is a clear violation of Christ's command that we do to others as we would have them do to us (Matthew 7:12). Furthermore, 1 Peter 3:1-2 reminds us that the best way to win our husbands (even unsaved ones) is most assuredly not through nagging: "Likewise, ye wives, be in subjection to your own husbands; that, if any obey not the word, they also may without the word be won by the conversation of the wives; while they behold your chaste conversation coupled with fear."

I've been in Bible studies where women used every opportunity to tear down their husbands. Often it was done in a joking manner, but that didn't take the sting out of the words. Matthew 18 applies to husbands as well as to others. If our husbands offend us, we are required to go to them privately to discuss the matter biblically. We should not rush to pick up a phone or log in and blog about their latest misdeeds! Far better to "cover all sins" with love, as Proverbs 10:12 instructs.

I love reading about our foremothers in the faith, and I've found so many who inspire me to be a better wife. These women cultivated deep relationships with their husbands, writing long and tender letters to them while they were away and building close, honoring relationships with them when they were home.

Abigail Adams wrote hundreds of loving letters to her husband and best friend, John Adams. In October of 1774 she wrote, "I dare not express to you at 300 miles distance how ardently I long for your return. I have some very miserly Wishes; and cannot consent to your spending one hour in Town till at least I have had you 12…"[51]

Later, in August of 1776 she confessed the deep passion she had for her very dearest of friends as she wrote to her beloved husband:

> I have spent the 3 days past almost intirely [sic] with you. The weather has been stormy, I have had little company, and I have amused my self in my closet reading over the Letters I have received from you since I have been here… Here I say I have amused myself in reading and thinking of my absent Friend, sometimes with a mixture of paine [sic], sometimes with pleasure, sometimes anticipating a joyfull [sic] and happy meeting, whilst my Heart would bound and palpitate with the pleasing Idea, and with the purest affection I have held you to my Bosom till my whole Soul has dissolved in Tenderness and my pen fallen from my Hand….[52]

Today's wives are told they cannot expect their husbands to be their best friends or to meet all of their needs. We are encouraged to seek out women friends who can share our woes, listen to our marital problems, and commiserate over the difficulties of bringing up children. We're supposed to schedule time to just "hang out," spending money or dishing the latest "news" over a cup of coffee. Of course, there is a place for relationships between women, but these cannot be based upon gossip, family disloyalty, shared bitterness, or unwholesome intimacy.

The relationships laid out for women in Scripture are based upon mutual edification, mature counsel, biblical wisdom, and genuine affection grounded in godly fellowship. But, even then, these friendships are not meant to compete with or take the place of the unique and precious relationship between husband and wife.

It's really very simple: God made man to need woman. It's hard to overemphasize this point. God gave Adam his calling, then showed him that he had no helper suitable for him (Genesis 2:20). Then God created Eve from Adam's side, making a helper who was an intimate part of him from the start—one who would find her calling in relation to his. Adam reacted powerfully and poetically when he received this beautiful gift from God. Eve wasn't just an adornment or a companion; she was his helpmate—one who would complete him and help him fulfill God's commands.

When a woman is truly one with her husband, his ideas, concerns, goals, and needs become hers as well. She becomes knit together with her husband as they labor in concert to build a godly family, open their home to saints and strangers, and reach out to their community. As the wife works hard in her role, her husband prospers in his, and they develop a lifelong friendship that cannot be matched.

We don't want to mold our husbands into the image of impotent androgyny; we want to encourage them to grow into the image of Christ, our Heavenly Bridegroom and King. The choice is ours. We can become the wise, capable helpers God created us to be, or we can tear down our homes with our own hands in a vain quest to "equal" men. God called femininity "very good" when He created Eve different from Adam; let us rejoice in that role and pour ourselves into servant-hearted submission to Christ as we bless our husbands.

Do you want to see your husband succeed and prosper? Do everything you can to build him up in his God-given role. Don't create extra burdens for him to bear; ease his burdens by capably undertaking your own role in the home. Don't compare him to other men or wish he'd change to please you; praise the good you see and thank him for what he does well.

With true masculinity under attack in Western culture, make it a point to keep all the negatives outside your door; don't bring them into your home through attitudes or actions. "Let the wife see that she reverence her husband" (Ephesians 5:33). Let your children hear you praise your husband, and tell them what a wonderful father they have.

The more we take your eyes off our husband's shortcomings, the more wonderful qualities we will see. Many a marriage has been transformed by the simple application of God's command that wives submit to and respect their husbands. Remember that godly femininity complements masculinity— it brings wholeness to humanity. It doesn't compete. It doesn't seek its own glory but delights to see others succeed and earn praise. And in doing this, godly femininity receives the greatest praise of all from godly masculinity:

> *Her children arise up, and call her blessed; her husband also,*
> *and he praiseth her. Many daughters have done virtuously,*
> *but thou excellest them all. Favour is deceitful, and beauty*
> *is vain: but a woman that feareth the LORD, she shall be*
> *praised. Give her of the fruit of her hands; and let her own*
> *works praise her in the gates.* (Proverbs 31:28-31)

Chapter 8

The Dangers of Whitewashed Feminism

Stacy McDonald

Feminist philosophy, which sounds reasonable enough on the surface, is a subtle and pervasive poison, infecting the minds of Christians and non-Christians alike.
—Elisabeth Elliot

L ike a filthy and unruly stray dog on bath day, feminism has been scrubbed and perfumed and presented to us as biblical. However, just as bathing a dog doesn't baptize him into the faith (he is still a dog, after all), neither does sanitizing the corrupt philosophy of feminism make it Christian. You see, it is possible to be a Christian feminist, but ironically there is no such thing as "Christian Feminism." The Christian feminist is either herself deceived, or she is attempting to deceive us (2 Peter 2:1-3).

Even though this chapter isn't meant to be a formal critique of feminism, we can still pull back the curtain a bit to expose its deceptive nature—even in its seemingly milder and perhaps more seductive form. Disguised as a sympathetic champion fighting against female oppression, the enemy has led many women (even Christian women) astray by whitewashing a pervasive evil—feminism, in all its ugliness.

G.K. Chesterton once said that the "chief object of education is not to learn things but to unlearn things." Since most of us have been brought up in a society already entrenched in humanistic, egalitarian thought, it's not surprising that we have feminist baggage we need to rid ourselves of. Even those of us who would recoil in horror at being thought of as a "feminist" battle the same old urge that Eve did: we, that is conservative Christian women, still struggle with the desire to be in control.

Because feminism has permeated almost every area of our culture, it is important for us to view all we believe under the scrutinizing lens of Scripture, diligently searching God's Word to see "whether these things are so" (Acts 17:11). We must beseech God to cleanse our hearts and minds of worldly ideals concerning womanhood and replace them with His standards:

> *And be not conformed to this world: but be ye transformed by the renewing of your mind, that ye may prove what is that good, and acceptable, and perfect, will of God.* (Romans 12:2)

The Secular Feminist: "Not the Fun Kind"[53]

Few topics evoke more emotion in women than feminism, and yet not all feminists look the same or share the same goals. Feminists sport a variety of public fronts.

In examining the feminist landscape, a number of observers have divided feminists into two primary camps—secular feminists and evangelical feminists. While other designations might be offered, for the sake of our discussion we will examine the feminist playing field based on this grid.

First, there are "secular feminists."[54] These are women who reject Christianity outright and deny the authority of Scripture. Self-proclaimed feminists who fall into this category tend to be stridently pro-abortion and militantly demand equal status with men in the workplace, and beyond.

Some of the most extreme "secular feminists" are lesbians and outright misandrists—women who hate men. This is the far end of the "secular feminist" spectrum which most of us picture when we hear the word *feminist*: the stereotypical, bra-burning radical who brazenly denounces men.

While I have encountered a handful of professing Christians who take this radical posture, they are the exception, as most women who claim the name of Christ reject this brand of feminism as extreme.

The Evangelical Feminist: The Whitewashed Kind

On the other hand, there is a more clandestine form of feminism which has crept into many modern churches. Observers have dubbed its adherents "evangelical feminists."[55] These feminists claim to hold Scripture in high regard, yet they do not accept the biblically defined role distinctions between men and women, and they reject male authority to varying degrees. While some "evangelical feminists" *admit* to their belief in the limited authority of the Scriptures regarding their role, others simply try to twist the Bible's meaning to fit their lifestyle. This more subtle version of feminism is particularly dangerous due to its beguiling cloak of Christianity, because, at its core, it is no different than its "secular" counterpart. While its face may be more polished and its manifestation less extreme, in essence, it is nothing more than whitewashed feminism.

Many whitewashed feminists, consistent with their egalitarian beliefs, advocate the ordination of women in the church. Others, no doubt weakened in their feminist resolve by the unyielding truth of Scripture, rightly agree that women should not be ordained in the church. Yet somehow they still insist on reinterpreting the passages that teach differing roles for men and women in the family. Ultimately, they reject the wife's biblical mandate to submit to her husband as her head.

Consequently, the biblical directives given to women to be wives, mothers, and keepers of the home are minimized or set aside as quaint but unnecessary options. Although they still view homemaking as a legitimate life choice, in their opinion it certainly shouldn't be viewed as *enough* and definitely not best. We're told women should want more. Peter's instructions to Christian women to be "meek and quiet" and "in subjection to their own husbands" (1 Peter 3:4-5) are regarded as weak and outdated by many, while more aggressive traits are admired: being ambitious, domineering, independent, and demanding.

While the whitewashed feminist may claim Christ, she does not fully embrace the Scriptures—she picks and chooses which of Christ's teachings she feels like following. This is dangerous indeed.

Feminist Heresy: Errors in the Bible?

Mary A. Kassian, in her book *Women, Creation, and the Fall*, describes the whitewashed feminist this way:

Biblical feminists view the Bible as open to alteration. One of the basic presuppositions of Biblical feminist theology is that the Bible is not absolute and that its meaning can "evolve" and "transform." Since the Bible presents no absolute standard of right and wrong, feminists maintain that they must decide this for themselves. This basic premise allows them to interpret the Bible in any manner appropriate to their immediate circumstances.[56]

In his revealing book *Evangelical Feminism: A New Path to Liberalism*, Wayne Grudem describes how feminist Paul Jewett teaches that "the apostle Paul's advocacy of female subordination in marriage and the church was a remnant of his rabbinic training that he had not fully resolved when he wrote his epistles."[57]

In other words, Jewett believes the words the Apostle Paul wrote in Scripture, which described a woman's role, were corrupted by the oppressive and demeaning view of women Jewett claims was characteristic of the Jewish scholars the Apostle Paul studied under. So according to Jewett, although Paul was a fine apostle, some things he wrote in the Bible are wrong.

In his book *Finally Feminist*, egalitarian John Stackhouse makes the same proclamation. He asserts that Scriptures reflecting non-egalitarian teaching can be discounted because they are based on Paul's human "limitations" or our misunderstanding of Paul's alleged doubletalk.[58] He claims to agree with the complementarian—that Paul *meant* it when he told wives to submit to their husbands—but then sides with the feminist by clarifying that the apostle only meant "for right now" (i.e., during a temporary period when patriarchy[59] would be a necessary evil).

Stackhouse's version of the roles of men and women is an evolving one. He believes that feminism is something that God has chosen to hide since Creation, and only now (since egalitarianism is becoming more prevalent) are we able to hear His fuller truth on this matter.[60]

Similarly, Asbury Seminary professor Dr. David Thompson claims the Apostle Paul was wrong in his interpretation of Genesis 2 given in 1 Timothy:

> *Let a woman learn in silence with all submission. And I do not permit a woman to teach or to have authority over a man, but to be in silence. For Adam was formed first, then Eve. And Adam was not deceived, but the woman being deceived, fell into transgression. Nevertheless she will be saved in childbearing if they continue in faith, love, and holiness, with self-control.* (1 Timothy 2:11-15, NKJV)

Thompson writes, "We should take caution in immediately assuming that Paul's reading of Genesis 2 must, without further inquiry, be ours." He goes on to say:

> It is entirely possible that at this point the creation account, understood on its own terms, must be the arbiter of the more specifically confined reading given by Paul.[61]

Grudem reminds us to notice what's happening here:

We are interpreting Genesis 2. And though Thompson may claim that Genesis 2 becomes the judge of Paul's interpretation, the actual result (in the article) is that Thompson's interpretation of Genesis 2 becomes the judge by which Paul's interpretation is pushed aside. Thompson's argument means that our interpretation can correct Paul's interpretation of Genesis 2—and, by implication, we could eventually correct Paul's interpretation of other Old Testament passages as well.[62]

Truth Be Told

The crux of the matter is this: feminists have trouble with Genesis 2 because it portrays a clear picture of the biblical roles in marriage *before* there was any sin. When Paul quotes from Genesis 2 to confirm male-headship in the church, he is proving that God's created order was established in the *beginning* and was not to be abolished. Paul said, "For Adam was first formed, and then Eve" (I Timothy 2:13). The order of the sexes is not the result of the Fall, but rather the result of God's order of creation. Hath God said, or not? To be consistent, feminists must nullify the inerrancy and sufficiency of Scripture and allow every other part of God's Word to be brought into question as well.

Though Matthew Henry didn't have the benefit of living in such "enlightened" times as ours, he certainly seems to understand the beauty and truth found in 1 Peter 3:1-6:

> Of Sarah, who obeyed her husband, and followed him when he went from Ur of the Chaldeans, not knowing whither he went, and called him lord, thereby showing him

reverence and acknowledging his superiority [authority] over her; and all this though she was declared a princess by God from heaven, by the change of her name, "Whose daughters you are" if you imitate her in faith and good works, and do not, through fear of your husbands, either quit the truth you profess or neglect your duty to them, but readily perform it, without either fear or force, out of conscience towards God and sense of duty to them.[63]

The Beauty of Completion

Feminism, blatantly secular or whitewashed, demands that we turn a cold shoulder to the beauty and grace of God-ordained womanhood and instead embrace the hollow barrenness of "personhood." To follow this concept to its logical conclusion, we would also have to reject the complete truth that God fashioned Eve from Adam's own rib and presented to him a suitable helper (Genesis 2:21-24)—a "good" gift—a wife who complemented him perfectly (1 Corinthians 11:2-16), and we must instead convince ourselves that God made for him a great partner—an interchangeable, androgynous roommate!

But this is not what the Bible teaches us concerning the order of marriage from Creation. The plain text of Scripture tells a different story:

> *"And the Lord God said, 'It is not good that man should be alone; I will make him a helper comparable to him.'"*
> (Genesis 2:18, NKJV)

On the day God designed them male and female, He demonstrated Eve's intrinsic worth in that she, too, was created in the image of God (Genesis 1:27). Yet, even at Creation, God revealed the role He had planned for her—a "helper" to her husband—the finishing touch to the masterpiece of oneness designed to take dominion over all the earth and multiply generations who would glorify Him!

The one-flesh unity that Scripture describes is one of the wonders of God's Creation (Genesis 2:24). God's Word has revealed to us a deep mystery concerning the sexual union of a husband and wife—an unfathomable truth that our minds are expected to conceive in faith and our spirits are to absorb. As we contemplate the sheer glory of our Lord, we can't completely grasp such an awesome thought as Christ's own intimate relationship to His Bride—the Church. The oneness described in Genesis pales in comparison to the inestimable oneness that will be experienced by us on that glorious day when our Groom returns for His spotless Bride (Ephesians 5:27).

In her essay "The Essence of Femininity," author Elisabeth Elliot laments the blindness of the feminist to the beauty of the complementary roles in God's creation:

> Why must feminists substitute for the glorious hierarchical vision of blessedness a ramshackle and incoherent ideal that flattens all human beings to a single level—a faceless, colorless, sexless wasteland where rule and submission are regarded as a curse, where the roles of men and women are treated like machine parts that are interchangeable, replaceable, and adjustable, and where fulfillment is a matter of pure politics, things like equality and rights?[64]

As the heavens declare the glory of God, so too do the

very bodies of men and women. Just as a man gazes across the Grand Canyon or scans the microscopic universe found in a drop of ocean, we can, on a much grander scale, stand in awe of the harmonious makeup of God's created order—a created order that He called "very good" when it was finished, not an incomplete creation that had to evolve to reach perfection.

The design of our physical bodies testifies to the fact that though men's and women's bodies are very different, they fit together in a way that brings glory to His name. A woman's body is intricately designed to receive the seed of man and, by the power of God's gift of life, conceive and nurture the next generation (Psalm 139:13-16).

Although whitewashed feminists understandably don't wish to be lumped together with the radicals, that connection is inevitably made when they resist their scriptural roles. One cannot be a partial feminist any more than one can be "kind of pregnant." Once conceived, it is only a matter of time until the labor pains begin giving birth to rebellion against God's creation order.

As whitewashed feminism infiltrates the church, there is a growing trend for spiritual teachers to legitimize the sins and weaknesses most common to women: rebellion against proper male authority, independent power and ambition, and a desire to be something God never intended for her to be (Genesis 3:5). I encourage Christian women to carefully analyze their thinking and cautiously choose the books they read, blogs they visit, and teachers from whom they choose to learn. As the Apostle Paul warns:

> *Beware lest any man spoil you through philosophy and vain deceit, after the tradition of men, after the rudiments of the world, and not after Christ.* (Colossians 2:8)

Try Walking a Mile in My Shoes!

While affirming male authority as outlined in the Scriptures, I am not discounting the genuine cases of despotism. Some men have abused their power and neglected to lead and protect their families. Some husbands and fathers are lazy, selfish tyrants. These men have not lived with their wives in an understanding or loving way, and, by their abuse[65] and neglect, they have harmed their own families and helped to debilitate society. Their prayers have undoubtedly been hindered (I Peter 3:7).

But regardless of whether or not men obey God by faithfully *leading* and loving their wives, as women, we are still required to obey God by faithfully and respectfully *following* our own husbands. Our responsibilities to the Lord aren't contingent upon the obedience of anyone else. We are to submit to our husbands "as unto the Lord" (Ephesians 5:22).

Even when husbands fall short, God can use the faithfulness of godly, submissive wives as a catalyst for change. Peter says it can be done without a word—by our *chaste* and *reverent* behavior (1 Peter 3:1-2),

> *Even the ornament of a meek and quiet spirit, which is in the sight of God of great price. For after this manner in the old time the holy women also, who trusted in God, adorned themselves, being in subjection unto their own husbands.* (1 Peter 3:4-5)

If a Christian wife is called to submit even to a heathen husband, how much more should she submit to an imperfect Christian husband?

Whatever trial we are experiencing, we can be sure that God is at work in us. We must not reject the trial or irritation, because it is God's will for us at this point in our lives. When we recognize it as being from His hand (for our good and His glory), we can accept even our trials as precious gifts—wonderful opportunities to testify of His goodness.

Matthew Henry reminds us, "We must abide by this principle (Psalm 17:14) that whatever it is that crosses us, or is displeasing to us at any time, God has an overruling hand in it."[66]

Thayer's definition of meekness says, "Meekness toward God is that disposition of spirit in which we accept His dealings with us as good, and therefore without disputing or resisting."[67]

It is so hard not only to say we accept His dealings with us as good, but to truly believe it! Matthew Henry describes meekness as "easiness." Another word would be forbearance or acceptance. Here is a portion of what he shares:

> There is meekness toward God, and it is the easy and quiet submission of the soul to his whole will, according as he is pleased to make it known whether by his word or by his providence...Meekness is easiness (forbearance) for it accommodates the soul to every occurrence, and so makes a man easy to himself and to all about him...[68]

"To all about him"? Would this include our husbands? Do we make it easy for our husband to lead us and our children?

Then again, Henry shares nuggets of convicting wisdom regarding "quietness":

> Inferiors are commonly very apt to complain. If everything be not just (fair) to their mind they are fretting and vexing, and their hearts are hot within them; they are uneasy in their place and station, finding fault with everything that is said or done to them…
>
> Those unquiet people whom the apostle Jude in his epistle compares to "raging waves of the sea, and wandering stars: (ver. 13), "were murmurers and complainers" (ver. 16), blamers of their lot, as the word signifies. It is an instance of unquietness to be ever quarrelling our allotment. Those wives wanted (lacked) a meek and quiet spirit who "covered the altar of the Lord with tears" (Mal. 2:13). Not tears of repentance for sin, but tears of vexation at the disappointments they met in their outward condition.[69]

Do we find ourselves weeping tears of repentance over our own willfulness and disobedience, or are we too busy weeping tears of bitterness over our husband's sin or neglect?

When we repent of our blindness to our own sin and willfulness and lay down our desire to rule, we will be free to rejoice and thank God for His provision and cling to the role He has given us—praising God that we are liberated from the bondage of sin that makes us loathe submission to our husbands.

But, I'm Not a Feminist!

As tempting as it is to listen to the popular mantra of modern society, we must stand firm in the truths of Scripture. Too many times we unwittingly soak up the pollution of the world (Matthew 12:43-45) because our spirits are empty of God's Word (Proverbs 15:28; 1 Peter 3:15). We therefore find ourselves ruled by our flesh rather than by the Spirit of the living God.

Suffragist Elizabeth Cady Stanton was an example of a discontented housewife who was ruled by her flesh. In a letter to her close friend and fellow suffragist, Susan B. Anthony, Mrs. Stanton complained:

> I pace up and down these two chambers of mine like a caged lion, longing to bring to a close childrearing and housekeeping cares. I have other work at hand...Oh how I long for a few hours of leisure each day. How rebellious it makes me feel when I see Henry going about where and how he pleases. He can walk at will through the whole wide world or shut himself up alone, if he pleases, within four walls. As I contrast his freedom with my bondage, and feel that because of the false position of women I have been compelled to hold all my noblest aspirations in abeyance in order to be a wife, a mother, a nurse, a cook, a household drudge, I am fired anew and long to pour fourth from my own experience the whole long story of women's wrongs.[70]

Most women reading this book would not consider themselves feminists. Nonetheless, many of us still struggle with some of the same attitudes described by Mrs. Stanton. As much as we hate to admit it, as women, we all have feministic tendencies. It is part of our sin nature—the flesh we battle on a daily basis.

Instead of learning to die to self and follow Christ wherever He may lead, many times we demand our own way. We feed the flesh until it has an uncontrollable appetite with a mind of its own—pulling us in the direction of whatever feels good for the moment—led by our own carnal desires. Ironically, it's an illusion, because the closer we get to what is supposed to "feel good" the worse we actually feel, the more we want, and the more our character suffers.

Matthew Henry once wisely said, "Virtue is a penance to those to whom home is a prison." If we view our God-given role as a punishment to women and the domesticity of the home as a cage, we—like poor Mrs. Stanton—will indeed find ourselves in misery and lacking the virtue needed to truly love, obey, trust, and serve the Lord.

There are those who believe that when a woman submits to her husband she somehow loses her identity. They claim that when a woman believes it is her glorious duty to keep her home serving her husband and children, she has, in essence, become a doormat. Ironically, by rejecting God's ways, that's exactly what the enemy intends for us to become—self-created doormats!

Many women naïvely follow individualistic feminist thought right into the arms of corporate America. Instead of being servants to their families, they become slaves to a system that cares nothing about them. In their delusion, they believe they are finally free. What they don't realize is that Satan stands laughing as he wipes his feet on their precious "personhood."

Patrick Henry once said, "It is when people forget God that

tyrants forge their chains." Satan knows that if he can keep us focused on *our* rights and all those needs that supposedly aren't going to be met unless "*we do* something," we'll be so distracted that we'll miss the good part. If he can keep us looking out for Number One and running away from servanthood because we fear becoming slaves to "some man" and a bunch of clinging children, then he can clamp shut the shackles!

> *And whoever of you desires to be first shall be slave of all. For even the Son of Man did not come to be served, but to serve, and to give His life a ransom for many.* (Mark 10:44-45, NKJV)

True freedom comes from having the liberty to obey God (Romans 6:16). "Whom the Son sets free is free indeed" (John 8:36)! Freedom doesn't come from being enlightened. One doesn't shake loose the chains of bondage by "finding" one's self. We have the ability to embrace the "good life" because the Lord of lords chose to die for us. Real life comes when we learn to lose ours—for His sake.

> *He that findeth his life shall lose it: and he that loseth his life for my sake shall find it.* (Matthew 10:39)

Chapter Nine

The Way Out: A Former
Feminist Looks Back

Jennie Chancey

In the summer of 2001, I received a wonderful letter from a
pastor's wife in Oregon. She had read *Mother*, by Kathleen
Norris, which I'd edited for republication the year before, and
wanted to share some anti-feminist literature she'd collected.
That little packet of information she sent sparked the idea
that became Ladies Against Feminism (LAF), the website we
started in order to expose the dangers of feminism and praise
the beauties of biblical femininity. Since launching the website
in 2002, the response has been overwhelming. Hundreds of
ladies from all over the world have contributed articles, links,
and testimonies. Many have sent in personal stories of their
journeys out of feminism.

But LAF's beginning was far more personal for me. What
you need to know is this: mine is not a story of perfection. I
was once a Christian feminist; I've seen the other side. I know
how empty it is. I've done my share of straying, most of it
due to my own pride. I went from die-hard homemaker-in-

training to dedicated career woman—and then God gripped my heart. My journey into and back out of feminism is one that took me from a rich home life to the lonely pinnacle of barren "accomplishment," then back again to a blessed home and family.

LAF exists to warn others away from the pit I fell into—to avoid the folly that once gripped me. I don't want other women to make the same mistakes I did and waste years trying to put together the broken pieces afterwards.

From Home and Hearth to Self and Career

From toddlerhood, I wanted to be just like my mother, the most capable, intelligent, and creative homemaker I've ever known. I also wanted to be a writer like my father, a celebrated aviation historian who wrote prolifically and managed to have a real life at the same time, always putting people before projects. Both of my parents invested in me—my mother teaching me how to manage the home, cook, sew, design my own patterns, practice hospitality, and so much more; and my father encouraging my love for writing and teaching me even to enjoy the process of editing (something I loathed for years).

As homeschoolers, we had the opportunity to pack our books and travel the world with my father as he took on various aviation-related writing projects. I devoured literature and art in Great Britain, marveled at biology in South Africa, and consumed volumes of history all over the United States and Canada. Such educational freedom was a great gift and fed my love of learning *and* my love for my family, because we were able to do all these wonderful things *together*.

Yet, just five years after graduating from high school, I'd already sold my birthright and turned my back on home. What could have caused such a solid, family-focused, homeschooled Christian girl to do such a thing? The change wasn't overnight and didn't seem dramatic to me at the time. I was like the proverbial frog in the pot of lukewarm water. By the time the water was hot enough to cook me, I was already comfortable and hadn't noticed the change.

With my high school diploma behind me, I really wanted to stay home and continue studying under my father to hone my writing skills while helping my family, but my parents wanted me to go to college. So, after a year's sabbatical, I decided to stop dragging my feet and make the best of things. I jumped into my freshman classes with enthusiasm, determined to make good grades and do my parents proud. In a small Christian college, I nevertheless encountered humanism and feminism in many of my classes.

I burned up the phone lines the first few weeks of one of my Bible classes. My professor had earned his doctorate by "proving" that the Bible didn't actually forbid women to teach or have authority over men (1 Timothy 2:12). I was flabbergasted. Scripture was crystal clear on this point. Tellingly, this professor never once brought up 1 Timothy but based his entire thesis in 1 Corinthians 14:34-35[71]. According to this professor's interpretation (backed by novel findings of evangelical feminists), Paul wasn't issuing a command at all. Instead, he was quoting something the Corinthian men had said in order to refute it. In other words, those foolish Corinthians thought women couldn't teach in church, but Paul disagreed and mocked them for their backwardness. I wondered why it had taken nearly two thousand years for someone to figure out that Paul meant the opposite of what he had written, but I held my tongue in class and called my parents instead. I never thought to bring up 1 Timothy 2 during Q&A. My professor had a doctorate. Maybe he knew something I didn't.

Pastor Brian Abshire has written about this very phenomenon in Christian colleges. He notes that even conservative Christian colleges are rife with liberal teachings, because the professors they hire come out of universities that demand doctrinal compromise:

> [E]very single faculty member I ever had in Christian college and seminary bore the scars from their highly regarded, Ivy League secular graduate programs. It is not that they "lost" their faith, but that they had been compromised...What [all colleges] share in common is the insistence that their professors have accredited degrees from prestigious universities; universities that have already abandoned the faith. Does anyone else see a connection here? The students pick up the errors of their professors, and when *they* become professors, pass those errors on to their own students. And after a couple of generations, we have to start all over again.[72]

So instead of fighting the onslaught of novel interpretations and clever feminist hermeneutics, I took copious notes and diligently worked for the coveted "A" in every class. I thought I was finally becoming sophisticated and erudite. A steady undercurrent flowed through every class and seasoned conversations with peers: "You're on your own now; time to grow up and be your own person." But my newfound superiority did not immediately squelch my relationship with my family. I still called home nightly, craving my parents' counsel and company.

Coming from a close-knit family, I found it completely natural to talk with my parents about everything and ask them questions when I ran into difficulties with professors or classes. But as the weeks passed by, I began to see that this idea was frowned upon in the college atmosphere. Peers wondered why I called home so much. Wasn't I glad to be "free"? My freshman orientation class focused upon cutting home ties and learning to make decisions and stand alone. My parents had certainly prepared me to follow good study habits, monitor priorities, and choose friends wisely, so this advice was easy to follow. But the whole notion of basically cutting off regular communication with home was foreign to me.

Slowly but surely, the message sank in: "This is about *your* life and *your* future; you've got to choose your own path now." My calls home dwindled. Before long, I began to enjoy the fact that I could do what I wanted to do when I wanted to without asking anyone's permission. I was a "good girl," always completing my studies before pursuing other activities, because that was just common sense. But with each passing day, my family sank into the distant past, and I saw myself as an individual, my future unconnected with anyone else. This individualistic shift in my foundation paved the way for everything else that followed.

The early protests I'd felt against feminism and humanism in the classroom softened. As each semester passed, I objected less and less. I felt I was finally learning to be grown up as I stopped fighting ideas that would have repulsed me only a short time before. Tellingly, I didn't talk with my parents about my shift in beliefs. Slowly, the "no way!" of my freshman year became the "why not?" of my sophomore year and, finally, the "it must be so" of my junior and senior years. I turned less often to the Lord for answers to my dilemmas. As I did so, my bitterness and disappointment with life grew, though I didn't realize at the time that my disillusionment was directly connected to my changing worldview.

Even though I spoke with my parents infrequently, I still loved them and was happy to see them when I went home. I respected their advice, though I often tempered it with my own "wisdom." Living in the self-contained universe of the campus, it was very easy to play at adulthood. I truly believed I was in the "real world" and learning to make it on my own. That notion makes me laugh now. What "real world" provides you with a room, three square meals you don't have to cook (on dishes you don't have to wash), an entertainment committee to make sure you have enough movies and concerts to attend, a library stocked with books centered on your own particular interests, free fitness facilities, and more? This was "individualism" without the price tag. Oh, and pay no attention to that cook (and dishwasher and janitor and maintenance man) behind the curtain.

So I continued in my quest to be my own person and build a future for myself. I scoffed at the girls who had come to college for their "MRS" degree, choosing to forget that I'd harbored secret hopes of meeting Mr. Right, marrying, and starting a family myself. That last stubborn brick in my original foundation had to go: my love for family—particularly my respect for my parents and my desire to be like them.

Toward the end of my college career, I met someone who began to chisel away at my admiration for my parents. When I talked about my parents' extremely close and happy marriage, this man told me I was deceived. No one was truly happy in marriage. In fact, a man's wife is never enough for him; he needs other lady friends to give him the things his wife cannot.

As far gone as I was at that point, I found this idea shocking and sickening…at first. How could any man claim to need other women to fill up the "blanks" his wife should be filling? I thought about my parents and their genuine love and friendship. I thought of their loving attitude toward one another, of my mother's respect for my father, and my father's high regard for my mother. It just couldn't be so! Dad had never needed another woman! I felt sorry for this man's wife who must have to compete with other women for his attention.

But, over time, like Chinese water torture, the bitter words began to seep through my psyche. Doubts planted as tiny seeds grew into monstrous weeds, filling me with apprehension. *Did my father really love my mother?* If men need other women besides their wives, then what is the point of marriage? Before long, I thoroughly doubted my parents' honesty. *They must be putting up a good front*, I thought. *Probably so we children will feel secure. But they can't be happy—not really happy.*

It was at this point that I decided marriage wasn't for me. Even though I loved my father and brother, I decided the majority of men in the world were self-centered jerks. All my dreams of marrying and having lots of children were silly anyway, right? Hadn't I just invested in four years of "higher" education? Why should I waste all my talents and gifts on being "just" a homemaker? So I hardened my heart and reinforced my image as "ice queen." I congratulated myself on my individualism. Who needed a family?

I came out of college having accepted a lot of "truths" that I didn't take the time to investigate thoroughly. I just gave up the battle and embraced them because everyone else was doing it. I bitterly accepted the fact that this was the way the world worked, whether I liked it or not. I traded my belief in the family as the bedrock of society for a belief in radical individualism—whatever works for you must be right. I would have been well served to remember Proverbs 28:26: "He that trusteth in his own heart is a fool: but whoso walketh wisely, he shall be delivered." But I'd forsaken the Source of wisdom and decided I could forge my own path.

I exchanged my abiding faith in godly marriage for doubtful distrust in my own parents and other godly couples around me. They were all just fooling themselves. No one person could ever be my best friend and lover all rolled into one. *That* was a fairy tale, and I was no Cinderella.

I had become a full-fledged Christian feminist. I tried to soften my image by calling myself "empowered," insisting that following my own heart and doing my own thing were still somehow biblical. But deep down, I knew what I was doing was feministic at heart. I was doing *my* thing, *my* way, and on *my* time-table.

I traded my admiration for my mother's accomplishments for a determination to succeed on the world's terms, which meant a nice paycheck and all the goodies that went along with a career—the meals out, the designer clothes, the shiny car. I never stopped to consider the irony of women measuring themselves in terms of their earnings—how was being a wage slave under a boss better than being a free woman under a husband?

Doubts niggled, but I strangled them. Deep down, I really didn't want a career, but I wasn't about to say that to anyone. Not after all that had been spent on *me* in time, effort, and money. So I got a job in media relations, putting my writing and editing skills to use and spending eight-hour days in a windowless office. This was not what I'd imagined my life would be like back when I was a carefree 17-year-old, traveling by my father's side and eagerly filling journal pages with my reflections, dreaming of my future life as a wife and mother. But this was the real world, after all, and I figured I'd better embrace my "empowerment" and get to work. I devoured books on "equity feminism" and took my stand in that camp. After all, they didn't burn bras or hate men, so I could be a feminist, after all.

Tipping the Sacred Cows

But God wasn't finished with me, and I've never stopped thanking Him for that. He began bringing people into my life who gently tugged at the blinders I'd put on in college. I saw husbands and wives who deeply loved each other and had vibrant ministries through their homes. I met daughters who served in the local church with incredible ability and, yes, *joy*. Most of all, though unknown to me at the time, my parents prayed fervently for me and admitted to friends that they had unwittingly pushed me into feminism. Behind my career-woman armor, the ice started to melt.

God opened my eyes to the results of feminism's teachings—both in society and in the Church. The love for history that had been instilled in me by my father became one of the tools God used to open my eyes. I began reading about the history of early feminism in the eighteenth and nineteenth centuries and became disturbed as I saw the correlation between women rejecting the biblical model and the rise in destructive behaviors and attitudes. I studied Marxism and Communism, stunned to see the clear parallels between those anti-Christian philosophies and feminism. Writer after writer documented the long-term damage (culturally, economically, and spiritually) of the feminist movement, including "no-fault" divorce, rampant promiscuity, children brought up outside of the family in daycare, growing consumerism, loss of home care for elderly relatives, and the list goes on.

The more I examined (and cross-examined) the evidence, the harder it became to hold on to any brand of feminism, "conservative" or otherwise. I read of scores of young women rejecting the egalitarianism of their parents in favor of strong marriages and childrearing at home—often to the dismay of their more liberal parents. I read exposés of the daycare movement by both secular and religious authors who demonstrated that children need married parents and stable homes. I read of young people embracing purity in a culture of promiscuity.

In all of these cases, I noted with amazement that what both secular and religious writers were urging (whether or not they openly acknowledged it) was a return to the biblical model of marriage, child-rearing, and family welfare. Yet their words seemed to fall on deaf ears, as Western civilization continued to decline.

Then it hit me: the Church today is jumping on a train whose engine has already gone over the cliff! Instead of getting out and turning around, we've decided the train car will be just fine if we paint it a prettier color or call it by a different name. But feminism is still feminism; and the results of feminism will be just the same for the Church as they have been for the world—possibly worse, because we should know better.

Quite simply, there is no such thing as "Christian feminism." We either embrace the biblical model and call it "very good" (just as God did after He created it), or we reject it and plummet over the cliff with the rest of the passengers on the runaway railcar. Do we really need to lose a generation or two before we decide to stop this folly?

After trying all that feminism had to offer in the way of freedom, I found myself empty-handed and frustrated. "Equality" couldn't deliver on its promises, so I sought the truth from the only reliable Source we have—the Word of God. I didn't deserve the second chance God gave me, but when I saw the lifeline, I grabbed it with both hands and climbed out of a trap of my own making.

When the scales finally fell from my eyes, the first thing I did was to go to my parents and seek their forgiveness. I told them about the seeds of doubt that had been planted during my time in college and how I'd grown to distrust my own family. Mom and Dad were incredulous when they heard how I'd questioned their marriage. They wanted to know why I hadn't come to them immediately with my concerns. I could only shake my head and explain that, in my new found "individualism," I'd refused to check the facts and had swallowed the most preposterous lie instead. In retrospect, I could only marvel at my gullibility and my willingness to doubt my parents because of the bitter words and implications of one person.

Six months after I'd disowned feminism and repented to my parents, God brought into my life the man I would marry. Twelve years later, our love has grown and deepened, and we are the blessed parents of eight children. There are times I look around and catch my breath, thinking of all the wonderful lives that wouldn't be here if I'd embraced my barren "empowerment" and rejected biblical family life. God brought me full circle by showing me that individualism is merely an attractive lie. No one lives in a bubble. Decisions we make will, in time, affect other people, whether we like it or not. We are meant to live in community—not in isolation. When God said it wasn't good for Adam to be alone, He really meant it. Societies and cultures are not built on individuals; they are built on the strong families God creates from men and women who covenant with one another for life and bear fruit for His kingdom! God even promises to "set the solitary in families" (Psalm 68:6), providing a practical and beautiful way for us to live in community with the outcast, the widow, the orphan, and the stranger. This is the Body—not the individual parts, but the whole, knit together by our wise and loving Creator.

Finding the Way Out

If you've fallen into the trap I fell into years ago, there's hope! God's ways are not for perfect people; they are for us. They're for the ones who have failed, because God is both our Redeemer and our Friend. Read on, because this book is for those *in* the pit as much as it is for those who've never fallen in.

If you're standing on the edge of the precipice, listening to the siren song of feminism, let me urge you to stop your ears. The lure may be sweet, but the trap is bitter. I lament the years I wasted trying to "find myself" when I could have been dying to self. I regret the relationships I hurt while trying to prove myself to others when I should have been laying down my life for the brethren. You don't need to waste years just to see for yourself if the forbidden fruit is really rotten. Biblical womanhood has so much more to offer that you don't want to waste a minute of time throwing your gifts and talents away on pursuit of your individual goals. There is much to be passionate about as we pursue biblical womanhood! Kindling this passion and fueling it for the glory of God is our life's calling, and no side road (however tempting) is going to lead us to contentment and joy.

Whenever we are coaxed to follow our own understanding and trust our own judgment (or the judgment of a pagan culture), Scripture calls us back. It does not change, because God does not change. God was faithful to me even when I was unfaithful to Him. His grace reaches out to us no matter how we have failed. God is able to preserve His people, generation after generation, as movements rise and fall, as kingdoms and cultures come and go. Feminism is as old as the Garden of Eden and simply recycles the same tired line: "God was wrong; taste and see—I can give you something better." But Satan's rotten fruit will not satisfy our deepest hunger. That can only be filled by the passionate love of the Bride for her Groom as she serves Him with all of her heart. What a calling! And what a faithful God we serve, Who does not leave us to our folly but calls us out time and again. From wretched desperation to passionate adoration: it's the story of the Gospel! This is our heritage in Christ. Let us not forsake it.

> *Trust in the LORD with all your heart,*
> *And lean not on your own understanding;*
> *In all your ways acknowledge Him,*
> *And He shall direct your paths.*
> *Do not be wise in your own eyes;*
> *Fear the LORD and depart from evil.*
> *It will be health to your flesh,*
> *And strength to your bones.* (Proverbs 3:5-8)

Chapter Ten

Servanthood: Whose Slave Do You Think I Am?

Jennie Chancey

But God be thanked, that ye were the servants of sin, but ye have obeyed from the heart that form of doctrine which was delivered you. Being then made free from sin, ye became the servants of righteousness. (Romans 16:17-18)

Everywhere you go these days, it seems life is all about *you.* Signs declare, "Have it your way," "Get it now," "You're worth it," and other self-centered slogans. We've grown accustomed to getting what we want, when we want it, in a world of fast-food, instant money, and drive-through everything. Life runs on fast-forward in this world of the Self, as we ignore the needs of others in our rush to get the most out of our own lives.

But, as more and more people are finding out, happiness remains elusive, because there is no rest in the endless pursuit of self-gratification. Nothing ever satisfies when our goals are selfish, no matter how many new ideas we try. Movies and television project images of blissful people who have found just the right things to make them fulfilled, but it's an illusion played out by paid actors whose real lives are just as messed up as anyone else's. The truth is, if we constantly pursue our own happiness, we will never find it. It will always be a few steps out of our reach. Without biblical contentment, we can never find peace. We can run like rats in a maze, frustrating ourselves and others, and finding in the end that there is no cheese—only another maze.

How is deep, abiding contentment to be found? If it isn't in careers, riches, houses, a great spouse, or wonderful children, then where are we supposed to look? This is where God gives us the eternal paradox: true life is found in death; true happiness is found in sacrifice; true peace is found in giving away our comforts and security.

Jesus is Our Model

Jesus said, "I have come that they may have life, and that they may have it more abundantly" (John 10:10). But instead of asking how Jesus defines "life," we just run off in pursuit of our own abundance. How *does* Jesus define life? Just read a little further in the same chapter, and you find that Jesus came to lay down His life for His sheep. Later he says, "Greater love hath no man than this, that a man lay down his life for his friends" (John 15:13). Over and over again, Jesus shows us that true living is found in joyfully sacrificing ourselves for others. It is found in dying to our own desires and wants so that we can pour ourselves out for Christ in the service of others. St. Paul wrote, "[Christ] died for all, that those who live should live no longer for themselves, but for Him who died for them and rose again" (2 Corinthians 5:15).

This is where most of us have to admit we are ready to jump ship. *Sounds like slavery to me,* we think. *No, thanks. I give enough of myself as it is. I don't have the time or energy to give any more.* We miss the whole point that God doesn't give us a choice between slavery or non-slavery. He tells us we can be either slaves to sin or slaves to Christ! Christ bought us with His blood; we belong to Him. Fighting against this is folly. Here's where we kill contentment and push happiness away with both hands. We're so afraid of becoming the ever-dreaded "doormat" that we don't even want to consider that God's ways might just actually bring the joy, peace, and delight we vainly seek. It's time to confront our fear and trust God that what He says is true. It's time to be passionate housewives who take delight in serving and find that service beautiful and meaningful.

Being Mary in the Kitchen

Most of us know well the famous Bible story in the tenth chapter of Luke about Mary and Martha. As Martha busily went about preparing food and making all things ready to serve Jesus, Mary sat quietly at Christ's feet, joyfully listening to His words. Martha's frustration level rose as she grumblingly went about the housework, resenting her sister's apparent lack of consideration. I can picture Martha, banging jugs and plates in the kitchen, trying to give Mary a not-so-subtle hint that she needs help with the serving. Finally, Martha blows her top and stomps out to Jesus: "Lord, dost thou not care that my sister hath left me to serve alone? Bid her therefore that she help me" (Luke 10:40).

Now, if you're a hardworking homemaker, you might just sympathize with Martha. There she is, working hard to serve

Jesus in her home, and her lazy sister just sits around the whole time...right? But Jesus's gentle rebuke is for Martha—not Mary: "Martha, Martha, thou art careful and troubled about many things: But one thing is needful: and Mary hath chosen that good part, which shall not be taken away from her" (Luke 10:41). Ouch.

Now, I've actually heard people use this passage to justify not doing housework or serving in the home. I've read that Jesus is once for all doing away with women's roles in the home by demonstrating that it is more important to sit at His feet than to do housework. But that idea just won't jive. After all, someone *does* have to do the housework! Those meals are not just going to magically prepare themselves, nor will the table set itself or the dishes clean themselves afterwards.

Serving is a fact of life. Jesus' point here is not that no one should have been preparing a meal for Him or tending to household matters. As always, Jesus slices straight to the heart. Luke 10:40 says Martha was "distracted with much serving." Instead of rejoicing in the ministry of love and service she was pouring out to the Lord, she resented the physical work and her sister's lack of help. The "good part" of which Jesus spoke was worshiping and adoring Him—which is something we should do all day long without ceasing.

We can all be Mary, even if we don't have an hour to sit down for "quiet time." It's all in our attitude toward the things that need to be done and the people we are serving. If we view our husbands, families, and guests as so many leeches crying, "Give, give!" then we are not going to develop a godly joy as we serve them. If we resent the fact that our husbands sit down to read with the children while we are preparing supper, we are being harpies, just like Martha. Choose the better part. Be Mary in the kitchen. Sing praises while you sweep up those never-ending crumbs. Whistle hymns while you wipe down the bathroom. Meditate upon Scripture while you are folding that third pile of laundry.

I feel greatly blessed to have been brought up in a home where my father urged excellence in our work as a way of glorifying God and where my mother joyfully tackled the tasks that lay before her. Whether organizing cabinets, planning school projects, upholstering furniture, planting a garden, or welcoming strangers, Mom always made every job seem like an adventure. When we complained, she just sang louder or turned up the music so we could march around in time as we did our chores. As a result, my parents' home was fragrant with the aroma of servant-hearted, life-giving hospitality.

And let me just say it again: it wasn't because we had beautiful furniture, just-right curtains, or spotless rooms. It was because Christ was Lord of that house, and our job was to serve Him without being bitter or acting put-upon. Be a Mary! When the laundry piles rise up in rebellion, the children don't do their chores right, or the kitchen sink never seems to quite empty itself, rejoice! Choose the better part, crank up the praise, and lay down your life.

Me First, or Else

The buzz in Christian circles today is that women must put themselves first or they will simply burn out or become depressed. I've seen this in several Christian magazines and on big-name Christian websites. The reasoning goes, "If Mama is putting herself first and being fulfilled, then she'll be happier and will keep everyone else happy." I hope red flags go up immediately when you read unbiblical advice like this. While this might appeal to our egos or our self-centered sin natures, this is most definitely not biblical teaching. Let's look at what Jesus had to say about putting self first:

> *And he sat down, and called the twelve, and saith unto them, "If any man desire to be first, the same shall be last of all, and servant of all."* (Mark 9:35)

and

> *[W]hosoever will be great among you, shall be your minister: And whosoever of you will be the chiefest, shall be servant of all.* (Mark 10:43-44)

Now, I'll grant you that this is rank foolishness to the world. How on earth can anyone be happy if she is constantly putting herself last? Pop psychologists would tell you that you have a martyr complex and that you need to be liberated from servitude. But let me just testify to you that the Word of God is true and even *practical* on this point! Our selfish desires will only make us miserable if we cling to them.

When I look back over my life and remember unhappy times, I can always see that those were the times I was being most selfish and me-centered. We think we can be happy by getting our own way and doing what we want to do. But this simply isn't true. That's the fastest way to make ourselves miserable over the long haul. We find true satisfaction and delight when we pour ourselves out "like a drink offering" (Philippians 2:17) in service to others and trust Christ to do His will in us and through us.

People need the gospel, and they need to see it lived humbly and faithfully by Christians who love God's Word and embrace it without compromise. Having older women teach younger women to "love their husbands [and] love their children" is now a countercultural act. It is radical in the new cult of the Self. But it is not impossible.

It will mean rejecting materialism and seeing possessions as a means to bless others rather than to fulfill our own desires. It may mean giving up pet projects or personal ambitions. But what it means above all is a willingness to joyfully surrender to Christ, laying down our lives and serving in the indispensable role God has given us as women. It will mean training our daughters to seek the kingdom of God by rejecting selfish ambition and vain conceit. It will mean death to self.

It Sounds Impossible!

"But I'm not like you!" someone says. "I didn't grow up in a hospitable house, and I never learned to do the things that seem so easy for you." First off, thank God right now that you are you and not me. One of me is enough. Sister, I am a sinner *just like you.* I have my own set of monsters that like to come out of the closet at night and taunt me with my failures and shortcomings. You have different monsters, but to ask for mine is just plain silly.

God has put you in the family He chose, He has placed you where you live, He has made you a member of that imperfect local church body, and He is going to continually equip you to be a Mary in your own situation. Believe it! That's what sanctification is all about. God doesn't hit us with a magic wand and make us perfect overnight. It is to His glory that He doesn't, because we'd try to take credit if He did. That's our nature. We really want to feel that we are in some way responsible for all the good things we do. But it's all due to His grace and nothing else.

Next, look at Ecclesiastes 3:11-13, and take this passage to heart: "He has made everything beautiful in its time…I know that nothing is better for them than to rejoice, and to do good in their lives, and also that every man should eat and drink and enjoy the good of all his labor—it is the gift of God" (NKJV). Hear that? It is God's gift to us to do good—and to enjoy it while we're doing it! In fact, read that whole book of the Bible (in-between changing diapers, making meals, and wiping the crayon marks off the table!) I call the book of Ecclesiastes "The Homemaker's Handbook." Get it into your head and into your heart.

Life *is* full of seemingly futile and repetitive tasks. You aren't going to escape that fact, no matter how good you are at keeping house, feeding your family, and demonstrating hospitality to saints and strangers. But you do have a choice about how you will approach those tasks. You can choose to view them all as "vanity" (empty, wasteful, meaningless), or you can choose to view them as the "better part" that God has graciously given you (service to Christ, pathways to joy, and spiritually meaningful).

We need to realize that work is a gift from the Lord. He

gave Adam and Eve work to do before the fall, so work isn't the curse. Difficulty and futility in work is a curse, but it doesn't help things to gripe and whine. There are many women out there who are bedridden or disabled in ways that prevent them from working in their homes. That should really spur us on to do excellent work with thankfulness. Be thankful for your health, be thankful for the ability to get up in the morning, be thankful for the tools God has given you that are such a help. If our pioneer foremothers could successfully bring up ten children while boiling laundry, grinding wheat for bread, and keeping dirt floors clean, then what's stopping us? Don't fear hard work. Embrace it and learn to do it as unto the Lord.

Slaves to Christ, Not Slaves to Self

God's ways are not our ways, and what the Bible calls us to do is, frankly, backwards in the world's eyes. Be least in order to be the greatest? Die to live? Go last to be first? Christ's example is most convicting: God of creation and Lord of all, He made Himself "of no reputation, taking the form of a bondservant, and coming in the likeness of men. And being found in appearance as a man, He humbled Himself and became obedient to the point of death, even the death of the cross" (Phillippians 2:7-8). Want to be equal to God? Become a servant. Humble yourself. Wash the feet of complaining followers. Die to self daily. Do we love God's Word enough to be faithful to it even when it is difficult? Or are we only willing to embrace it when it makes us happy or fulfills a need? Jesus said that if we loved Him, we would obey His commandments—and not just the ones we like.

If we feel unfulfilled in the very moments of our daily lives, what is holding us back from contentment? My late father always told me I could choose my attitude each day. It was no one's fault but my own if I had a miserable day. I had the responsibility to reject sinful attitudes and embrace godly ones—on a daily (sometimes moment-by-moment) basis. I could get up angry with my lot in life and bitter toward God for putting me where I was, or I could get up, thank God for a new day, ask Him for help in turning from sin, and approach even the smallest tasks with a diligent joy. Sound crazy? It's not. It really does work—not by our power, but by the power of a faithful Lord who has given us His Spirit so that we may follow Him joyfully, even in the midst of trials.

> *Then shall the righteous answer him, saying, "Lord, when saw we thee an hungred, and fed thee? or thirsty, and gave thee drink? When saw we thee a stranger, and took thee in? or naked, and clothed thee? Or when saw we thee sick, or in prison, and came unto thee?" And the King shall answer and say unto them, "Verily I say unto you, Inasmuch as ye have done it unto one of the least of these my brethren, ye have done it unto me."* (Matthew 25:37-40)

Chapter 11

So Show Me What a Keeper at Home Really Looks Like!

Jennie Chancey

So, if a housewife isn't that stereotype of 1950s perfection in pearls and heels, then what *is* she? Down through the centuries, poets and artists have often idealized womanhood and created "pictures of perfection," as Jane Austen famously wrote.[73] The nineteenth century gave birth to stacks upon stacks of domestic "bibles"—books that detailed the duties of virtuous housekeeping and child training. While there is much to applaud in these poetic and practical paeans to femininity and domesticity, we are not attempting to resurrect old-fashioned ideals for the sake of "the good old days." What we really desire to do in this book is to present a full-orbed picture of *biblical* womanhood in all its beauty and complexity—and demonstrate why that picture is realistic and timeless rather than impractical and culture-bound.

Rest assured that biblical homemaking isn't about shiny appliances or weed-free flowerbeds (though those certainly might be some tools of the trade). It isn't about perfect children in neatly-starched clothes. It isn't about mealy-mouthed "yes-women" who never offer an opinion or share an original thought. Far from it! Biblical womanhood is challenging, intelligent, adventurous, kingdom-building, whole-hearted hard work. It encompasses all kinds of gifts and talents and provides us with an outlet for genuinely purposeful creativity and effort—all within the realm of the fully functioning Christian home.

To start us off, let me share what is by no means an exhaustive list of the traits and talents of the godly women we find in Scripture:

- Helping husbands take dominion through God-ordained roles and tasks (Genesis 1, 2; Acts 18:2-3)

- Serving as midwives (Genesis 35:17; Exodus 1:15-21)

- Playing musical instruments (1 Samuel 18:6; Psalm 68:25)

- Singing (Nehemiah 7:67; Luke 1:46-55)

- Feasting before the Lord with God's people (Deuteronomy 31:10-13; 1 Samuel 1:1-9)

- Demonstrating hospitality to strangers and saints (Genesis 18:6; Acts 16:15; Romans 12:13; 1 Timothy 5:10)

- Serving God's prophets (1 Kings 17; 2 Kings 4:8-38)

- Thinking quickly and resourcefully in the face of danger (1 Samuel 25:3-42; Judges 4:18-22, 9:52-53)

- Providing wise counsel (Judges 4:4-9; Proverbs 31:1, 26)

- Facing death for the sake of God's people (Esther)

- Weaving; creating works of art (Proverbs 31:13, 19)

- Crafting beautiful garments (Proverbs 31:22)

- Producing items in the home for the marketplace (Proverbs 31:18-19, 24)

- Assisting her husband with the family business (Acts 18:3)

- Augmenting the family estate through wise purchases and use of materials (Proverbs 31:16)

- Planning wisely for the future (Proverbs 31:21)

- Selecting with skill the food the family eats (Proverbs 31:14)

- Giving to the needy (Proverbs 31:20; Acts 9:36)

- Being the fruitful mother of many children (Psalm 128:3; Genesis 24:60)

- Teaching children with wisdom (Proverbs 1:8 and 31:1, 26; 1 Timothy 5:10; 2 Timothy 1:5)

- Training the next generation of women in a hands-on manner (Proverbs 31:15; Titus 2:3-5)

- Creating clothing for the poor (Acts 9:36-41)

- Opening the home to the Church (Romans 16:1; Acts 16:14-15)

161

- Supporting the work of the Gospel (Luke 8:1-3; Romans 16:6, 12)

- Privately exhorting fellow believers (Acts 18:26)

God has a *lot* for us to do! His work for women isn't small or narrow or confining. It calls forth the best in us and requires the faithful use of the talents He bestows. At the same time, God desires us to do His work *His* way. He had a plan for femininity when He called it "very good" in the Garden of Eden. Masculinity isn't enough, and there is no "rugged individualism" in the Bible—for men or women. When we chafe at femininity, we ultimately struggle against God's created order, which is *His* design—not the design of some Jewish male chauvinist six thousand odd years back.

There is a beautiful purpose in our femininity, and once we start to see how our traits complete—not compete with—the traits of masculinity, we should rejoice to fill the position God has called us to: helpers with a mighty role to play in the Kingdom of God. There's nothing "little" about it!

Homemaking isn't about starched aprons, pearls, and high heels. It's about doing the will of God even when the world scoffs. It's about loving the high calling that God especially has given to women. It's about learning to trust when circumstances would tell us to doubt and fear.

We are called to be different—not conformed to the pattern of this world but transformed by Christ (Romans 12:2). We are to live in such a way that others may have hope. When we trust in the Lord and submit to His design for marriage, family, home, and church, then our homemaking accomplishes far more than just making homes. It has the power to impact countless lives and generations for the glory of God.

A Real-life Example, Please?

My mother is one of my greatest heroines. I have always looked up to her as the personification of Proverbs 31. She would be quick to point out that she is no superwoman and never "did it all," but my childhood memories are filled with her creativity and productivity. She reminds me that she did things "in due season," meaning only when it was the right time to do them—which often meant saying "no" to some projects or dreams. But saying "no" to some things always meant the ability to say "yes" to others, and all those "yeses" made life inspiring and beautiful for everyone who came under my parents' roof.

To give you a small idea of how talented my mother was (and still is), I'll tell you that she could sew anything she saw a picture of, built me a dollhouse when I was eight, taught herself to upholster furniture (and briefly had a home business doing that when my siblings and I were small), painted in oils, refinished flea market finds, made soft-sculpture dolls (another home business in which I joined when I learned to sew), designed and planted intricate flower gardens around our home, harvested and canned vegetables, made jams, designed the passive solar home that we built when I was twelve, laid tile, painted and wallpapered rooms, made quilts, baked bread, created meals from scratch, invited scores of people into our home for short and lengthy stays, hosted several girls from Brazil to help them with their English (she is fluent in Portuguese, having grown up on the mission field in Brazil), edited most of my late father's books and magazine articles, homeschooled three children while traveling all over the States and in several foreign countries with my dad, and—here's a zinger—took a ride with Dad in a MiG-29 jet in Russia, the first American woman ever to do so!

Mom did all this in her role as helper to my father. She did not seek her own ends or insist on doing things her way. She did not mope about all the things she might be missing out in the "real" world. She did not envy my father in his work or seek to compete with him for attention or honor. She made her top priority the faithful, productive ordering of home life so that my father did not have to do double duty. And she *loved* to help my father succeed.

Mom's life has been anything but dull. She has amazing hands—hands that have seen a lot of hard work and never held back from doing their best. She has never met a stranger. She loves people, and people love her. She opens her home and her heart to those around her. This lady is amazing! I am so thankful that I grew up under her skilled teaching. Because of her, I never thought the term "homemaker" was derogatory or demeaning. How could it be, with a mother as capable and creative as my mom?

There's a funny story here, too. My mother once participated in a Bible study with several older women. These women were quite liberal in their beliefs and insisted all those teachings in Proverbs 31 and Titus 2 were purely cultural and time-bound and didn't apply to modern-day Christians. Mom quietly disagreed, stating that true freedom only comes from submission—to God first, then to a husband.

Jaws dropped all around the room, and one attendee burst out, "Why, Bettie! You are the most *liberated* woman I've ever known! Just look at all the things you have done!" My mother smiled and looked around at the shaking heads and shocked expressions. "That's just the point," she replied. "Submission is the freedom to be creative under a God-given authority! Submitting to my husband does not stifle my gifts; it puts them to their best use. My husband wisely directs the projects I undertake in the home and helps me to see when I am taking on too much. He knows my talents and can often tell me how best to use them." Heads continued to shake all around the room. One after another, these older women confessed frustration with their "equal" marriages and marveled at my mother's contentment and joy as a submitted wife.

My parents were not perfect, but they modeled godly marriage to their children on a daily basis. My mother always honored my father and never said anything against him before us children or anyone else. She praised him publicly. She led others to admire his work. She supported all of his projects and served as his secretary. Mom's respect for Dad led my brother, my sister, and me to respect and honor him, too.

In turn, my father loved and cherished my mother, praising her talents to anyone who would listen. He marveled at her ability to take a junky flea-market find and turn it into a beautiful piece of furniture. He loved her ability to make a small meal stretch to serve unexpected guests. He sought her opinions on everything. In short, Mom and Dad were a perfectly matched team. She joyfully helped him in her role, and he credited her with his successes. There was never a power struggle, because

Mom knew that real power comes from submitting to the will of God and accomplishing it *His* way in *His* time.

Every Home Will Look Different

Now, I'm not saying that a woman can't be a "real" homemaker if she doesn't oil paint or run a successful home business! The point here is not to make my mother the ultimate standard of homemaking but to give you a real life example of how one woman submitted to her husband without fear and then watched the Lord use her talents to bless her husband, family, church, and community. You may have a completely different set of talents, and that is fine. You may feel you only have one or two gifts. That doesn't mean you're inferior or can never hope to do great things for God in your role.

Christ praised the servant who turned two talents into four just as highly as the one who turned five into ten. The number of talents or the "wow" factor in increasing them has nothing to do with it; simple faithfulness to the Lord is key.

The beauty of God's design for home and family is that it doesn't involve cookie cutter Christians. In fact, this is His design for the entire Body of Christ:

> *For the body is not one member, but many. If the foot shall say, "Because I am not the hand, I am not of the body;" is it therefore not of the body? And if the ear shall say, "Because I am not the eye, I am not of the body;" is it therefore not of the body? If the whole body were an eye, where were the hearing? If the whole were hearing, where were the smelling? But now hath God set the members every one of*

them in the body, as it hath pleased him. And if they were all one member, where were the body? But now are they many members, yet but one body. And the eye cannot say unto the hand, "I have no need of thee": nor again the head to the feet, "I have no need of you." Nay, much more those members of the body, which seem to be more feeble, are necessary: And those members of the body, which we think to be less honourable, upon these we bestow more abundant honour; and our uncomely parts have more abundant comeliness. For our comely parts have no need: but God hath tempered the body together, having given more abundant honour to that part which lacked. That there should be no schism in the body; but that the members should have the same care one for another. And whether one member suffer, all the members suffer with it; or one member be honoured, all the members rejoice with it. Now ye are the body of Christ, and members in particular. (1 Corinthians 12:14-27)

I know families whose children form a talented string quartet; my children can barely plunk out a few songs on the piano. I know mothers who have painted breathtaking oil portraits of their children; my children are impressed if the little stick figures I draw actually have noses and ears! I know families who grow all of their own organic produce in abundance; I am happy if I can prevent my front flower bed from baking in the Alabama heat.

The point here is that God is going to equip every family differently so that His Body overflows with gifts on every hand (or foot!) I don't despair over my lack of artistic brilliance or fret because I have a black thumb. I rejoice when I see these talents at work in other women and families.

Your home is not going to look like mine, and mine is not going to look like yours. Even if both of us are faithfully and joyfully obeying God's commands, the results are going to be marvelously different. This is how God grows the Body with its diversity of gifts and talents. The eye doesn't do it all and cannot say to the hand, "I don't need you." And the hand can't boast that it doesn't need the foot, either. With the gifts God bestows on each of us (large ones, small ones, amazing ones, humble ones), we can glorify God together as a Body joined to our Head, Christ.

So forget about trying to copy exactly that wonderfully talented mother you know in your church or community. By all means, be inspired by her and seek to imitate her as she imitates Christ (1 Corinthians 11:1), but don't think you've got to do everything she does the way she does it in order to earn the "well done" of Christ. Take the gifts the Lord has graciously given to you and your family and cultivate them together for His kingdom.

But Where Did All the Older Women Go?

I get letters from dozens of young wives and mothers who struggle to obey the Bible's commands without a living example before them. All of them ask, "Where are those Titus 2 ladies who are supposed to teach us?" Many find that women whose children are grown leave home to pursue careers or outside interests and are too busy to instruct a young wife. Reading books on Titus 2 is not the same as having an older mother in the faith to lend a hand.

One older woman wrote me to ask if she had a role to play now that her children were grown. She wondered if she was meant to spend the rest of her days twiddling her thumbs or waiting for needy people to drop into her lap. Surely God had *something* for her to do!

The answer to both of these dilemmas is to bring these two groups together. Young women need the instruction, correction, and training of the generation that has gone before them. Older women need to give their time, wise counsel, and encouragement to the generation coming up behind them. Titus 2 isn't just about a woman's role; it's about inter-generational relationships for the mutual benefit of both.

You see, the biblical model for the family isn't "nuclear" at all. God is concerned with much more than one husband and wife and their children under a single roof. He has created the extended family and the Church family so that the older generation can pass its wisdom on to those following after and so the younger generation need not "reinvent the wheel" when it comes to living out God's commands in a fallen world in a practical way.

God's Word isn't about theories and spiritual niceties; it is vitally, sensibly down to earth. Revering the "hoary head" isn't just about showing deference to the elderly; it's about knowing where to go when we need wisdom in the flesh. Having older women teach young women wasn't invented by some ancient patriarch to keep women tied down to the home; it's the biblical way to foster healthy relationships and communication as wisdom is transmitted from the experienced to the neophyte.

Our work isn't over when our children are grown; in some

ways, it's just beginning, since our experience (failures and successes both) can now be turned around to train the next generation of wives and mothers. Do we want them to tumble into pitfalls we've already learned to avoid? Do we want them to struggle because we had to struggle? Or will we inculcate the biblical gift of *helps*—the desire and ability to serve others as the Lord has sanctified us?

If you are an older woman, I encourage you to reach out to the generation coming up behind you. Be that loving Titus 2 mentor who can encourage young wives and mothers in their calling. If you are a younger woman, I encourage you to seek out older women as a miner digs for gold. Those "nuggets" may seem few and far between, but they are out there. Many of them are languishing in nursing homes or sitting in "Seniors" classes in your church right under your nose. Don't wait for them to come to you; find them!

Striving for the Goal in an Imperfect World

We need to dispel any notion that God's will and God's Word can only work in a perfect world. Well-meaning people have said that, in our day, we just can't expect all mothers to be at home full-time. I've been told that I'm "lucky" to have a husband who makes it possible for me to stay home. I have to wonder how such thinking got a foothold only a few generations after large families were the norm and when the majority of mothers stayed home. What "ideal world" do we imagine existed when God gave His commands for husbands, wives, and families?

When Paul wrote to Titus and Timothy, the Christian church was in its infancy. The Roman Empire ruled the world.

Christianity was considered paganism by the polytheistic Romans and Greeks. *Oh, sure, you can have Jesus; just don't say He is the only God. Acknowledge Caesar's lordship, and all will be well. Put your God on His own pedestal, but don't tell us our gods can't have theirs.* As the countless stories of martyred saints tell us, Christians didn't just go along to get along or make any attempts to be "relevant" to their society. Instead, they went against the grain, obeying God's commands even when it meant losing their homes or their lives. Nero burned them as torches to light his evening parties. Wild animals ate them in the arena as spectators cheered. Emperors passed edicts against Christ-worship, forcing the followers of Jesus into the catacombs for safety.

It was in the context of this "ideal" world that God commanded husbands to give honor to their wives and love them as Christ loved the church, while pagan men treated their wives as chattel and committed infidelity as a part of their religion.[74] It was during this tumultuous time that God commanded the older women to teach the younger women to love and submit to their husbands, to keep their homes, to love their children, to welcome strangers, to care for the poor, and to be focused, rather than frivolous. Together the husband and wife were to train up the next generation of Christians to embrace God's design for the family.

God gave His commands to a feeble people lacking much and expected them to obey Him with great joy—with a hopeful understanding that God would supply all their needs if they just did what He said. God is a Keeper of promises. When He tells us to be salt and light, we must stop trying to figure out ways to make ourselves palatable to the world's tastes. How will they find hope if we live hopeless of seeing God do what He promises? If the Body of Christ doesn't believe in and act upon the promises of God, then how can we ask others to do so?

I'm here to testify to the goodness of God and the beauty and wonder of following His ways. Am I sinless? Not on your life. Do my children obey perfectly? No, they don't. Are there days we lose perspective? Yes, of course. We're fallen human beings, after all. But the good news is that we've been bought with a price and that the One who owns us calls us His friends (John 15:15). His commandments are not burdensome, and when we throw ourselves wholeheartedly into following them, we find rest, refreshment, and encouragement along the way. This is our birthright as Christians. Let's not sell it for a mess of pottage. Let's not wait for a mythical "ideal world" to come along in which it will be easy to obey. Let's face the fact that the Christian life is going to involve hard work and start getting our hands dirty!

But My Situation is Different!

Perhaps you are one of many women living in a situation that is far from ideal. Perhaps it is difficult to make ends meet. Or perhaps you're trying to run a home without any training or encouragement from Titus 2 mentors in the faith. Maybe your husband isn't the easiest person to please—or maybe he's apathetic and offers no scriptural answers to your questions. Where do you fit into this picture?

First off, I hope you're able to see that none of us are waiting for our husbands to become Mr. Perfect (for that matter, we're not Mrs. Perfect, either!) We're also not waiting for our children to stop sinning, our house to clean itself, or our church to overflow with godly grandmas who want to bring pies and friendship to our back door.

The answer is not a new self-help book, a wonder drug, or the newest self-esteem boost. The answer is often the last thing we want to find and the first thing we'd like to ignore. The answer is submission to Christ's loving commands—yes, even when it seems impossible and daunting and fraught with difficulty on every side. The thing all of us have to learn to do over and over again is to come to Christ, "casting every care upon Him, for He careth for you" (1 Peter 5:7).

I think this is sometimes the hardest thing to get through our heads. We often demand concrete, practical answers—a five-step formula or a set of actions that will guarantee results. But God so rarely works that way. Yes, His Word is jam-packed with practical and concrete commands, but it is also full of calls to trust, to lay down our burdens, to let go of our fears. I think this is a tall order for most of us. I speak from experience. There are times I've cried out to the Lord for help only to receive no easy answer. It has only been in hindsight that I've been able to see that what I took as a "no" was the Lord's gracious working out of His will over time and in a way I did not expect. These times of stretching are seldom easy, but they do sanctify us:

> *For which cause we faint not; but though our outward man perish, yet the inward man is renewed day by day. For our light affliction, which is but for a moment, worketh for us a far more exceeding and eternal weight of glory;*

while we look not at the things which are seen, but at the things which are not seen: for the things which are seen are temporal; but the things which are not seen are eternal. (2 Corinthians 4:16-18)

Now don't think I'm encouraging you to wish for a fairy-tale ending to your story. This is not about lightly dismissing real difficulties with a call to just stop worrying. You may still worry; I'm simply urging you to give that anxiety and stress over to the Lord and trust Him to move in His time. He is "able to do exceeding abundantly above all that we ask or think" (Ephesians 3:20), but there are also times He wishes to sanctify us through difficulties.

I often think of the Israelites who lived in captivity for generations. The temple had been destroyed; they could not go to Jerusalem to offer the sacrifices God had commanded them to give; they lived under a pagan government and no longer enjoyed the freedom of God's perfect law in a land of their own.

But instead of despairing and giving up hope, they submitted to God's yoke and continued to teach their children about the Lord's ways. God even commanded them to thrive in captivity, saying, "Build ye houses, and dwell in them; and plant gardens, and eat the fruit of them...And seek the peace of the city whither I have caused you to be carried away captives, and pray unto the LORD for it: for in the peace thereof shall ye have peace" (Jeremiah 29:5, 7). We can bear fruit and have peace even in seasons of "captivity." Give your situation over to the Lord, and do your best to submit to and honor your husband in difficulty. Know that the prayers of other women are with you.

I've heard many working women say that they feel condemned by their sisters in Christ. I've never met a homemaker who made catty remarks about or felt superior to a sister in the workforce. I suppose those women might exist, but Stacy and I aren't two of them! We've experienced the chastening hand of the Lord in our lives, too, and we are thankful that He doesn't ask us to be perfect before He will consent to use us. He takes us where we are and continually molds us into His image, promising to finish the work He has begun in us (Philippians 1:6).

Do you remember the widow of Zarephath? After Elijah hid in the wilderness and was fed by ravens, God commanded him to go to a pagan city to find a widow there who would sustain him:

> *And when he came to the gate of the city, indeed a widow was there gathering sticks. And he called to her, and said, "Please bring me a little water in a cup, that I may drink." And as she was going to get it, he called to her and said, "Please bring me a morsel of bread in your hand." So she said, "As the Lord your God lives, I do not have bread, only a handful of flour in a bin, and a little oil in a jar; and, see, I am gathering a couple of sticks that I may go in and prepare it for myself and my son, that we may eat it, and die." (1 Kings 17:10-12, NKJV)*

The widow had come to the end of her rope, so to speak. She couldn't see a way out of starvation and death. Yet the Lord sent Elijah, who told her to make cakes for him, for herself and her son, and he promised that the oil and meal would not run out. She submitted, and each morning, there was still just enough meal and just enough oil to last the day. God provided for her needs on a day by day basis, and when she cried out to Him for the life of her son, He restored him from death.

What seems impossible to us must have seemed doubly so to a pagan widow outside of Israel. Yet the Lord was faithful to the widow of Zarephath. He will also be faithful to you. There's no need to be desperate. Trust him as you submit to what seems an impossible yoke to bear, and let the peace of God rule in your heart. Pray continually, and ask the Lord to work through your circumstances. He is the God of the impossible.

Teach me, O LORD, the way of Your statutes,
And I shall keep it to the end.
Give me understanding, and I shall keep Your law;
Indeed, I shall observe it with my whole heart.
Make me walk in the path of Your commandments,
For I delight in it.
Incline my heart to Your testimonies,
And not to covetousness.
Turn away my eyes from looking at worthless things,
And revive me in Your way.
Establish Your word to Your servant,
Who is devoted to fearing You.
Turn away my reproach which I dread,
For Your judgments are good.
Behold, I long for Your precepts;
Revive me in Your righteousness.
(Psalm 119:33-40)

Chapter 12
Aspiring to Great Heights
Stacy McDonald

"For His own glow-y," the three-year-old future theologian recited.

Carolyn laughed and brushed her son's cheek. "Yes, Joshua, that's the right answer; God made you and all things for His own glory!" The little boy squeezed his eyes shut and gave her a silly smile. He was learning about God from his favorite place—Mama's lap.

"Okay guys, let's go in the kitchen. You can have a snack while Mama starts dinner," said Carolyn as she pulled out a container of leftover chicken. With dinnertime approaching, she decided to cut up the chicken, toss it with some pasta, and make a salad. "Who wants to wash and spin the lettuce for me?"

"I do!" several voices volunteered.

Carolyn still wasn't sure what was so exciting about using a salad spinner; maybe Grandma should buy salad spinners for birthday presents instead of Legos®! She chuckled as she imagined her mother's response.

"Okay, Matthew, after your snack I would like for you to wash and spin the salad."

She turned to her four-year-old, "Sarah, finish your snack, then fill the water pitcher and put it on the table for me, please."

"Yes, ma'am," Sarah piped.

Heading to the kitchen, Carolyn breathed a happy sigh as she passed the sailing ship made of a laundry basket, an empty wrapping paper roll, and a baby sheet. "What an imagination!"

"Jacob, please put away your ship. You can keep the paper roll under your bed and play again later, but now I'd like you to go fill the basket with clothes from the hamper and bring it to the laundry room."

"Yes ma'am. May I have my snack when I'm finished?"

"Go ahead and have your snack first; just don't forget the laundry."

"Yes ma'am; thank you," he chirped, bounding to the table for some fruit and cheese.

Carolyn watched her rollicking brood as they chattered around the table, and she silently thanked the Lord for His grace. She thought back to the days when her attitude had almost blinded her to the true blessing each of them were.

"What's wrong, Mama?" eight-year-old Matthew asked, noticing her serious expression.

"Absolutely nothing, honey; I was just thanking God for His grace and mercy…and for champion salad spinners like you!" she laughed.

The ring of the doorbell added to the noisy merriment around the kitchen table. The children, all eager to see who was coming for a visit, followed Carolyn to the door. The youngest children peered from behind their mother as she opened the door to find their neighbor, Leslie Brown, waiting with her dog.

"Why, hello; you must be Mrs. Brown! I believe my husband met your husband yesterday at the mailboxes. He said you might be by today."

"Hello; yes, I'm Leslie Brown. I hope I'm not disturbing anything." She looked around, hesitating.

"Not at all," Carolyn laughed, "come on in; we were just finishing up dinner preparations. I'm so glad to finally meet you. These are our children: Matthew, Jacob, Sarah, Joshua, and this is our youngest little guy, Benjamin. Children, this is Mrs. Brown."

"It's very nice to meet you, Mrs. Brown," the children said in staggered unison.

"Yeah, great to meet you, too," responded Leslie in a startled tone. She wasn't used to being introduced to children.

Carolyn motioned for the two of them to sit down on the couch. The children all sat on the floor around Leslie, squealing and waving at her little dog.

Leslie glanced at the stack of children's books on the table. "I knew you had lots of kids, and I thought one of them might be interested in babysitting my dog, Cindy, while I'm away. I hope it won't be too much trouble; she's a very good dog, and I'm willing to pay you."

The children all gasped in anticipation. "Can we please, Mom? I'll do all the work!" Matthew implored. He had been hoping to prove to his mother he was responsible enough to have a dog of his own, and this seemed like the perfect opportunity.

"Hold on, children," Carolyn laughed. Turning to her neighbor, she continued, "Well, as you can see, you have willing workers! I'll check with my husband, but I'm sure we can work something out. Are you going on vacation?"

"No, I'm the Director of Marketing for CarnArch Industries. My boss is sending me to Bangkok for two weeks to train our overseas team," Leslie explained. "I may be heading over to Singapore for a few days before coming home, so it could be that I'll need you to watch her for as long as three weeks."

"Wow, that's quite a trip! Would you like us to take care of your mail or anything?"

Leslie seemed distracted. "Are all of these children really yours?" she asked.

"Yes, every one of them; they're all keepers!" Carolyn joked.

Leslie seemed to be lost in thought for a moment. Catching herself, she straightened abruptly and smiled. "I'm glad that works for you," she asserted. "I never wanted children myself."

"Well, I must say I'm glad your parents did!" Carolyn replied with an encouraging smile.

Leslie shrugged, "Actually, I come from a large family; I'm the youngest of six. My father wasn't home much, and my mom was a talented seamstress who always felt frustrated that she never did anything with her life. As soon as I entered high school, my mother went back to school to get her degree in fashion design."

"So, what does your dad do?" Carolyn questioned attentively.

"He manages a chain of department stores," Leslie continued. "They're divorced now. As soon as we were grown and out of the house, my mom left my father."

"I'm so sorry; that must have been hard."

Leslie shrugged, "They had to do what made them happy."

"Excuse me a moment." Carolyn turned to six-year-old

Jacob, "Will you please go finish the salad for Matthew? And make sure you wash the cherry tomatoes, too. Daddy will be home soon. I would like Mrs. Brown's dog to have a chance to get used to Matt."

"But, *Mom*, I wanted to play with the dog, too; why can't Matthew do the salad? You told him to do it earlier," Jacob complained.

Carolyn calmly took her son's hand and looked him in the eye: "Jacob, you are back talking; that equals disobedience. You will finish the salad and wait for me in the kitchen."

"Yes, ma'am," Jacob sighed, shuffling toward the kitchen.

A little embarrassed, Carolyn apologized for the interruption and turned her attention back to her neighbor.

"Wow!" Leslie interjected. "My sister's kid would have thrown a fit! I can't believe your son walked into the kitchen so easily."

Surprised, Carolyn laughed. "Well, they're not perfect, as you can see, but God is showing us a lot of grace."

"You certainly have more grace than I would have," Leslie remarked.

Carolyn shook her head and smiled. "Well, it's not always been this way. There was a time when I thought my children would drive me crazy—I couldn't handle them; they seemed out of control. God had to show me that *I* was the one who needed changing. And with His help, I'm able to deal with each situation—to direct my children to love and obey God. And as you see, my children are still works in progress!" Carolyn chuckled, "It's a full-time job."

Leslie cleared her throat. "Hmm…that's interesting. I guess

it's a religious thing. Well, I'm glad you're happy, but I just can't imagine being home with kids all day—to not have time for myself. That's what happened to my mom." Leslie raised her eyebrows and shook her head.

Carolyn smiled again and quietly prayed for wisdom. "Well, I can understand your struggle. In fact, I learned the hard way that when I tried to serve myself, I only got further and further from what I was really after anyway. It was only after I poured myself into serving others—specifically my husband and children—that I found what I was after all along—a satisfied and meaningful life. The Bible teaches us to put others first. As a Christian, I finally learned this."

Carolyn wasn't sure where all this was going, but she was amazed at the opportunity God had given her to share how He had worked in her life.

"I just don't understand; how you can be happy serving other people all day," Leslie responded, a note of exasperation in her voice. "You seem like a smart lady; don't you ever worry about losing your identity?"

"Do you ever worry about losing yours?" Carolyn answered gently. "You work for a large corporation that doesn't know you as a person—doesn't really care. How would you like to work for your best friend all day? Imagine what it would be like to build a *real* empire together. Not an empire of stocks and bonds or skyscrapers, but future generations—something that truly lasts." Carolyn's eyes swept across the room where her children played.

Leslie followed Carolyn's glance, then shook her head and smiled wonderingly. "I've never met anyone like you," she said. "You really make it seem so wonderful—so different." She paused, then continued ruefully, "I have to admit, you're not really what I expected at all. At first, I thought I had walked into the home of June Cleaver, but you're obviously doing a lot more here than mopping and dusting."

Carolyn laughed outright, her eyes twinkling. "Well, thank you, Leslie! I take that as a supreme compliment! I do have a few pairs of high heels in my closet, but I can tell you that homemaking is a lot more than that old '50s stereotype!"

Leslie flashed a relaxed smile, then turned and patted her dog. "Well, I'd better be getting back home. Could you possibly let me know by tomorrow if you can keep Cindy for me?"

Carolyn nodded and stood up, holding out her hand to her visitor. "I'm really glad you came over today, Leslie," she said. "And I hope we can get to know you better in the future. Would you and your husband consider joining us for supper one night after you get back from your trip?"

Leslie seemed surprised but quickly recovered and shook Carolyn's hand. "That sounds nice," she said, noting the genuine warmth in Carolyn's eyes. "Yes, that would be really nice. Maybe when I pick up Cindy we could visit? That is, if it wouldn't inconvenience you...."

Little Sarah clapped her hands in delight and looked up at Leslie. "Oh, we just *love* having company over, don't we, Mama?"

Carolyn smiled at Sarah's enthusiasm. "Yes, we sure do!" she replied, as she led Leslie to the front door. Matthew reached out to give the dog one last pat as Leslie stepped over the threshold. The other children crowded in behind, calling out good-byes as Leslie waved and walked across the street.

"Thank you, Lord," Carolyn whispered as she closed the door and led the children back into the kitchen.

"What are you thanking God for, Mama?" Matthew asked, laying a cloth napkin over the prepared salad.

"For God's many kindnesses to us," Carolyn replied thoughtfully. "For giving your Dad and me you and your sister and all your brothers," she said as she hugged her son. "And for giving us real-life opportunities to bless others through our home."

While Carolyn's story is fictitious, it is true that our households can become real-life centers of gospel evangelism. Not only is the Christian home a haven where our children are to be brought up in the "nurture and admonition of the Lord" (Ephesians 6:4), but from our tables and firesides we can powerfully impact the spiritual lives of others beyond our family.

Years ago, I found myself on the receiving end of such a blessing. A simple family living a quiet life in the heart of Virginia noticed me in the midst of their everyday living. No fanfare, no sales pitch—just real-life Gospel-living. God providentially placed me in the path of Jack and Brenda Joyner at just the right moment—and I discovered the hands and feet of Christ living out the day to day.

This faithful wife revealed to me her true King, Jesus, by esteeming her earthly husband as "lord," in the way she lived out her days (1 Peter 3:6). She did not live her life as if it was her own, and as I watched her, I was utterly amazed. The joy that permeated her every nurturing act of service to her family confounded my selfish heart—and melted it. Not only was I ready to listen, but I begged for answers!

Her faithful husband, by mirroring the sacrificial love of a King for His Bride, revealed to me in living color Christ's sacrifice for the church. I was able to understand, at least in part, the mysterious love of the Gospel from this man living it out in his home with his wife and children. Love never fails! (1 Corinthians 13:8)!

No one handed me a tract or told me I was going to hell if I didn't repent. No one stopped me in the street to point to the burden of sin I carried of which I was already painfully aware. All those things could have been said; they were certainly true enough. Yet, I was shown the gospel by the winsome scent of hearth and home—and one true-to-life family living it out in all of its "everydayness."

A keeper at home is the true working woman. Properly managing a household is a demanding job; nurturing little ones, and caring for everyone's needs can be physically and emotionally draining at times. But for a wife and mother there can be no greater joy; no calling more satisfying; no occupation more dynamic.

Any task will have its mundane moments. Though you may experience "dry spells," take them as reminders to thirst after God (Psalm 42:11). When you are weak, remember to rely on His unending strength (Isaiah 40:29; 2 Corinthians 13:4) and plead for His mercy. When you are weary (Isaiah 40:31), run to your Savior where you will find rest and help in your time of trouble (Psalm 46:1).

We've discussed the truth of the great Gospel paradox—die to live. Now let us put actions behind our resolutions (Matthew

16:25). Know that your true reward and ultimate joy will only be found in the heart of your giving; and it will be a reward grander and more lasting—deeper and more magnificent than any miserable trinket you could have obtained by seeking it for yourself.

Virtuous womanhood is a glorious lifework—one God deems praiseworthy in His own Word (Proverbs 31). I pray that our time with you has helped you to see your role in the home as the artistic sculptor of souls; the resourceful shaper of an expanding kingdom. May you turn your back on the hollow image of desperate home life the world parades before us and learn to view your own home as a place of life, hope, joy, and industry—a place where spirits are made full and lives are changed forever for the glory of God. It is our sincere hope that you have begun to see the great rewards that will follow when you as a woman embrace God's glorious vision for passionate homemaking—a vision that reveals the exquisite beauty of a calling He's created just for you.

Afterword

Why It Took Two and a Half Years to Write This Book

Jennie Chancey

Back in March of 2005, I called Stacy to tell her about an alarming trend I'd tracked within Christian circles. I had just finished reading a book that basically declared biblical womanhood impossible and urged women to "find themselves" and "do whatever made them happy." Several secular and Christian magazine articles echoed similar themes. What disturbed me most were the numbers of discontented women jumping on the bandwagon and saying, "This is what I want to hear. I am tired of living for others; time to live for me."

That's when Stacy told me about a book project she and her husband had just begun to outline. As she listed the proposed chapters, I felt my excitement grow. "This is fantastic, Stacy!" I said. "Your outline matches every single point I'd like to raise about these false teachers. I mean, where on earth is the *Gospel* in all of this 'me first' stuff?"

Stacy continued to share her vision for *Passionate Housewives,* and I told her about the many LAF (ladiesagainstfeminism.com) readers who had contacted me, asking for a biblical refutation of "All About Me" teachings. That's when Stacy invited me to co-author the book. I'd only been thinking of writing an article for LAF; a whole book sounded a little daunting. But Stacy said we could split the chapters up, and I said I'd talk with my husband and pray about it.

A few weeks passed, and after much discussion and prayer with my husband, I accepted Stacy's offer. I told her there was no way I could commit to writing chapters without cutting out all other writing projects, so any articles for *Homeschooling Today*® magazine (which Stacy aided her husband in publishing) would have to go out the window. I'd also need to put the LAF site on hold and take a sabbatical so that any "spare" computer time could be devoted to working on *Passionate Housewives Desperate for God.* Stacy agreed, and the adventure began. I shut down LAF, ignored all but urgent emails, and committed to get the writing done.

A few weeks later, I got a note from a longtime LAF reader who expressed concern about the book project. She felt that I would have to compromise my family in order to do this, and therefore that she couldn't in good conscience buy the book when it was published. I appreciated her concern and wrote her back. I also posted something on LAF after my sabbatical that I hoped would dispel any mistaken notions of what was going into the writing of *Passionate Housewives.*

When people hear the word "author," I think a mythical picture of a hermit-like writer, bent over a page in a dark room, shuttered away from everyone else for hours, days, weeks (months!) on end sometimes comes to mind. Let me shatter that myth very quickly, because I don't want anyone to imagine Herculean effort going into something that is no more involved than other pursuits like writing letters, talking to family members, or just living in a busy household.

I think it is important to explain that writing is not an "occupation" for me—any more than oil painting, flower arranging, furniture refinishing, or any other number of wonderful activities that are good and profitable (and that I totally lack the talent to attempt!) I guess you could say I write by the seat of my pants—on the fly; in spare moments at the end of the day; in my head when there's no time to jot things down; on the computer late at night when there is. My dear friend Stacy is the same way. With ten children, she isn't a "real" writer, either. That's the way we like it. We just write as grace allows. Nothing Herculean about it. Nothing amazing, or astounding, or genius-tinged.

When someone counsels me to give up writing altogether or risk neglecting my family, I don't brush aside the concern. But I also have to turn it around and apply it to just about every other activity in which I (or indeed anyone) can engage. You fill in the blank: "You need to give up _____ (talking on the telephone, writing letters, painting, musical instruments, gourmet cooking, sewing, gardening, walking, watching films, knitting, decorating your home, reading for pleasure, etc.) or you will end up neglecting your family." The truth is that *any activity* can distract us, pull us away from what is most important, or make us lose our focus.

You can put away any odd notions of the lone, romantic

writer, aloof from all earthly cares and caught up in a world of deep thoughts. It's nothing like that. It's much more like being in a very busy, noisy room and catching the occasional pause to file away a mental note or jot down a thought. That's life! I wouldn't have it any other way. Give me the rooms filled with giggles, spilled orange juice, piles of children's books, stray laundry waiting to be folded, sticky kisses, squabbles in need of mediation, and the general mayhem of a busy family that lives together all day, every day.

Plain and simple: Why did it take us over two years to write this book? Because we live in a real world full of real-life messes and mayhem. We hope you'll embrace that reality as well and thank God for everything that slows you down and forces you to contemplate your finitude. No superwomen here! Just a super God Who gives grace for every halting step we take.

About the Authors

Jennie Chancey

Jennie is the wife of Matthew Chancey and the happy mother of eight children, whom the Chanceys homeschool. When not cramming lots of reading into "spare" moments, she enjoys playing with her children, sewing, traveling with her family, and contemplating the mysteries of God's amazing universe. Jennie edits LadiesAgainstFeminism.com, a site which brings together writers from all over the world to expose the damaging effects of feminism and celebrate the beauties of biblical womanhood. She also owns the home-based Sense & Sensibility Patterns, begun when she was a newlywed to inspire women to embrace their femininity.

Stacy McDonald

Stacy is the thankful wife of Pastor James McDonald, the contented mother of ten children, a soon to be first-time grandmother, and the author of *Raising Maidens of Virtue: A Study of Feminine Loveliness for Mothers and Daughters*. She has been blessed with the opportunity to teach women around the globe on issues relating to the roles of a wife and mother, homeschooling, and Christian decorum. Stacy and her husband, along with their children, reside in Central Illinois and operate *Family Reformation*® ministries (www.familyreformation.org), dedicated to the reformation of the Christian family. To gain continued encouragement in your role as a wife and mother, visit Stacy's blog: www.yoursacredcalling.blogspot.com.

Endnotes

1   Gnosticism is an ancient heresy marked by a belief that all things within the physical realm are sinful. Note that God called all that He made during the Creation week "good" (Genesis 1:31), and that Adam and Eve could eat of every tree planted in the Garden of Eden, save from the Tree of the Knowledge of Good and Evil (Genesis 2:17).

2   A vernacular phrase that refers to a preoccupation with one's self. Derived from the word *omphaloskepsis*, which is the practice of contemplating one's navel as an aid to meditation.

3   Dorothy Patterson, "Where's Mom? The High Calling of Wife and Mother in Biblical Perspective," excerpted from *Recovering Biblical Manhood and Womanhood*, edited by John Piper and Wayne Grudem (Wheaton, IL: Crossway Books, 1991), p. 368. Hereafter cited as *RBMW*.

4   Simone de Beauvoir, "Sex, Society, and the Female Dilemma," *Saturday Review*, June 14, 1975.

5   Vivian Gornick, University of Illinois, "The Daily Illini," April 25, 1981.

6   Glenna Matthews, *Just a Housewife*. (Oxford: Oxford University Press, 1987), p. 219.

7   Here it is helpful to notice what God says is "good" (Proverbs 18:22) and what God says is "not good" (Genesis 2:18).

8   Doug Phillips, "Our Church Youth Group," <www.visionforum.org/issues/uniting_church_and_family/our_church_youth_group.aspx>, December 24, 2002.

9   Cheryl Mendelson, *Home Comforts: The Art and Science of Keeping House.* (New York: Scribner, 1999), pp. 9-10.

10   Matthew Henry, *Matthew Henry's Commentary on the Whole Bible: Complete and Unabridged in One Volume.* (Peabody, MA: Hendrickson Publishers, 1996, c1991), S. Pr 12:4.

11   Elizabeth Dodds, *Marriage to a Difficult Man: The Uncommon Union of Jonathan and Sarah Edwards.* (Laurel, MS: Audubon Press, 2003), p. ix of the foreword.

12   *Ibid.*

13   "A New England Village," Harper's New Monthly Magazine, <www.rootsweb.com/~maberksh/harpers/823.html>. November 1871, p. 823.

14   This quotation is taken from the Sarah Edwards Letter to her daughter Esther Burr, April 3, 1758, ANTS-FTL, Sereno Edwards Dwight transcription.

15   Timothy Lamer, "Unfocused Families," *World Magazine,* July 21, 2007.

16   Dorothy Patterson, *RBMW*, p. 369.

17   Edith Schaeffer, *A Celebration of Marriage.* (Grand Rapids, MI: Baker House Books, 1996), p. 84.

18   *Ibid.*, p. 85.

19   "The Estate of Marriage," sermon given by Martin Luther in 1522.

20   Quote from a letter Jane Austen wrote to her niece, Fanny Knight, March 23, 1817. *Jane Austen's Letters*, collected and edited by Deirdre Le Faye (New York: Oxford University Press, 1995), p. 335.

21   Louise Story, "Many Women at Elite Colleges Set Career Path to Motherhood," *The New York Times* (September 20, 2005).

22   Of the phrase, "For the present distress," Albert Barnes writes: "In the present state of trial. The word distress, αναγκην, necessity, denotes calamity, persecution, trial, etc. See Luke 21:23. The word rendered present, (ενεστωσαν,) denotes that which urges on, or that which at that time presses on, or afflicts. Here it is implied: (1.) that at that time they were subject to trials so severe as to render the advice which he was about to give proper; and, (2.) that he by no means meant that this should be a permanent arrangement in the church, and of course it cannot be urged as an argument for the monastic system. What the urgent distress of this time was, is not certainly known. If the epistle was written about A.D. 59, (see the Introduction,) it was in the time of Nero; and probably he had already begun to oppress and persecute Christians. At all events, it is evident that the Christians at Corinth were subject to some trials which rendered the cares of the marriage life undesirable." (Albert Barnes, *Barnes Notes: Notes on the New Testament.*)

23   *Ibid.*

24   See, for example, *Day Care Deception: What the Child Care Establishment Isn't Telling Us* (San Francisco: Encounter Books, 2003) and *Forced Labor: What's Wrong with Balancing*

Work and Family (Dallas: Spence Publishing Co., 2002)—both by Brian Robertson; and *Love & Economics: Why The Laissez-Faire Family Doesn't Work* by Jennifer Roback-Morse (Dallas: Spence Publishing Co., 2001).

25 "Mass Marketing, Technology Bring Security Home," (http://securitysales.com/t_inside.aspx?action=article&StoryID=1452).

26 "U.S. Service Industry Growth Revs Up to Highest in Year," (http://usmarket.seekingalpha.com/article/37436).

27 You can download this entire book for free from http://www.gutenberg.org/etext/15488.

28 There is a strange irony here that seems to be lost on us. American women in vast numbers now go out to work so that they can afford pay someone else to bring up their children, prepare the majority of their meals, clean and iron their clothing, and even plan and execute entertainment for their families. Most employees in these so-called "service industries" are women, who, in turn, must pay someone to bring up their children, cook their meals, etc. I am reminded of a childcare consultant quoted in Brian Robertson's book, *Forced Labor: What's Wrong with Balancing Work and Family* (Dallas: Spence Publishing, 2002): "The child care crisis is so acute that child care workers in many areas of the country are unable to find adequate day care for their own children" (p. 140). I'm tempted to pause and ask, "Hello? Anybody home?" This is a self-perpetuating problem. We've now built a culture that requires mothers to go and get jobs so they can pay other mothers bring up their children, while yet someone else is watching *those* children. It boggles the mind.

29 "Lycurgus was of a persuasion that children were

not so much the property of their parents as of the whole commonwealth…[N]or was it lawful, indeed, for the father himself to breed up the children after his own fancy; but as soon as they were seven years old they were to be enrolled in certain companies and classes, where they all lived under the same order and discipline, doing their exercises and taking their play together." (Plutarch, *The Comparison of Numa with Lycurgus* [ca. 800 B.C.], http://www.fullbooks.com/Plutarch-s-Lives2.html)

30   "When Christians arrived in Rome and its vicinity, they encountered another culturally depraved practice that showed its low regard for human life. If unwanted infants in the Greco-Roman world were not directly killed, they were frequently abandoned—tossed away, so to speak." (Alvin J. Schmidt, *How Christianity Changed the World* [Grand Rapids: Zondervan, 2004], p. 52.)

31   "Christians, however, did more than just condemn child abandonment. They frequently took such human castaways into their homes and adopted them." (*Ibid.*, p.53.)

32   "Most of our brothers did not spare themselves and treated each other with heroic love and goodness; they fearlessly assisted the sick, they carefully nursed and served them in Christ, they cheerfully died with them…sharing the sickness of others, voluntarily taking on themselves their sorrows…. [It] was entirely different with the pagans. They drove out those who began to get sick …they threw half-dead people into the streets." (Eusebius, *Church History*, VII 22.7-9.)

33   "[Housework] is peculiarly suited to the capacities of feeble-minded girls." (Betty Friedan, *The Feminine Mystique* [New York: W.W. Norton & Co., 2001 (1963)], p. 255.)

34   Blue Letter Bible. "Dictionary and Word Search for *oikourgos* (Strong's 3626)." Blue Letter Bible. 1996-2007, 23 Aug 2007. (http://cf.blueletterbible.org/lang/lexicon/lexicon.cfm? Strongs=G3626&Version=kjv.)

35   Biblical passages teaching headship for men and submission for women are "a temporary accommodation to certain functional differences between men and women in ancient patriarchal cultures." (Rebecca Merrill Groothius, *Good News for Women: A Biblical Picture of Gender Equality* [Grand Rapids: Baker, 1997], p. 38.)

36   The "metrosexual" phenomenon, largely guided by the homosexual community in Hollywood, encourages heterosexual men to embrace effeminate fashions and manners, becoming softer and gentler. This is a modern-day version of yesteryear's "fop" and is part of a larger cultural push for greater androgyny. It has its share of detractors in both liberal and conservative/religious camps, though it remains fairly popular in the media. *Queer Eye for the Straight Guy* is a popular television show that promotes homosexual men as advisers to heterosexual men on fashion and style to help them look like metrosexuals.

37   I hesitate to describe "hookups" in detail. If you want a thorough education in this latest cultural phenomenon, see Wendy Shalit's book, *A Return to Modesty* (New York: Simon & Schuster, 1999). Essentially, it is what it sounds like: casual, commitment-free sexual relationships outside the confines of any kind of relationship (including casual dating).

38   See *The War Against Boys: How Misguided Feminism Is Harming Our Young Men* (New York: Simon & Schuster,

2001) by Christina Hoff-Sommers—an equity feminist who nevertheless recognizes that it is not healthy to force boys to squash their masculinity and behave in feminine ways.

39   Egalitarianism is "a social philosophy advocating the removal of inequalities among people" (Merriam Webster's online dictionary [http://www.m-w.com/cgi-bin/dictionary?va=egalitarianism]). While we certainly agree that all people have the same inherent worth and dignity as human beings made in God's image, we do not believe that equality equals sameness or that it demands the elimination of role distinctions.

40   "Genesis 1 records that the human being was created in God's image and as male and female in that image (Genesis 1:26-27)…The second, and different, creation story of Genesis 2 shows that human being divided by God into male and female." (John Stackhouse, *Finally Feminist: A Pragmatic Understanding of Gender* [Grand Rapids: Baker Academic, 2005], p. 35. Hereafter cited as *Finally Feminist*.)

41   "The fundamental issue and danger of evangelical feminism lies in its methods of interpreting the Bible. These methods seriously undermine the credibility, integrity, and authority of God's written Word. They make the Bible an utterly confusing book, an unsolvable puzzle." (Alexander Strauch, *Equal Yet Different* [Colorado Springs: Lewis & Roth Publishers, 1999], p. 109.)

42   In 1923, the Southern Baptist Convention took a stand against feminism, publishing a book of essays by many prominent pastors and Baptist leaders. The book, *Feminism: Woman and Her Work*, edited by J.W. Porter, reveals that the "new" teachings of today are really recycled. We can truly

say with Solomon that "there is nothing new under the sun" (Ecclesiastes 1:9). Take this passage from a chapter titled "The Basis of Feminism" by Porter: "The advanced woman resents the fact that she is a woman. She rebels against the difference in sex and if possible would obliterate the fact that one is male and the other female. She is unsexed and would if possible break down all the barriers and distinctions of sex. She seems unmindful of the fact that we must reckon with the eternal 'he' and 'she.' In her grammar there is but one gender, and that is the neuter. There is no he or she, but simply and solely 'it.' Seemingly, she will never be satisfied until she can become the head of the family, provided of course, that there must be families. Her ambition appears to be to make herself independent of God and man…And here comes the tragedy of our civilization—the disintegration of the American home. The citadel of our civilization has been the solidarity and integrity of our homes" (pp. 22-23).

43   For a thorough treatment of pagan androgyny cults and practices and their revival in the twenty-first century, read "Androgyny: The Pagan Sexual Ideal" by Dr. Peter Jones (http://www.spirit-wars.com/articles.asp?section=Peter&id=96087).

44   "The reason for Paul's directives is not a domineering male chauvinism, but he desires that godly women assume their place in the spiritual battle…Intense conflict with the forces of darkness is waged in the home. Paul stations the godly woman in the home to engage in spiritual battle, to shore up the Christian family and fend off the enemy's slanderous attacks. His language is dignified, not derogatory. *Keep house* literally means 'house despot.' Here is a term which

legitimizes feminine authority and the power needed to direct the affairs of the home with a nobility bespeaking service to Christ. This is not relegating the wife to inconsequential." (Alan J. Dunn, *Headship in Marriage in Light of Creation and the Fall* [Demings Lake Memorial Church, 2001], p. 56.)

45   "Since Christ is a head, He perfectly models godly headship. Christ never abuses those under his leadership." (Alexander Strauch, *Equal Yet Different* [Colorado Springs: Lewis & Roth Publishers, 1999], p. 86.)

46   "The decline of fatherhood is a major force behind many of the most disturbing problems that plague America: crime and juvenile delinquency; premature sexuality and out-of-wedlock births to teenagers; deteriorating educational achievement; depression, substance abuse, and alienation among adolescents; and the growing number of women and children in poverty..." (D. Popenoe, "Life without Father," in C. Daniels, ed., *Lost Fathers: The Politics of Fatherlessness in America* [New York: St. Martin's Press, 1998] p. 33). There are numerous studies on the effects of fatherlessness. A quick online search will turn up dozens. The Alliance for Non-Custodial Parents Rights has posted many private and governmental studies on fatherlessness and divorce. They note that "society is just now beginning to recognize on a widespread basis what children have known all along—father-absence is one of the most destructive forces to children in our society" (http://www.ancpr.org/affects_of_fatherlessness_on_chi.htm). They quote from many studies and books across the spectrum, including the passage from *Lost Fathers* given here.

47   "In a culture which conveys messages to men

that they are not needed in distinctive roles of father and husband, many men leave their families or refuse to form families when they beget children. Gone are most vestiges of traditional stigmas once associated with divorce and out-of-wedlock births. We have forfeited much of the traditional wisdom relating child welfare to intact two-parent families. Fortunately, that traditional wisdom is now being supported by impressive social-scientific research. In the U.S., statistics that reveal the declining well-being of children chiefly point to two related causal factors: (1) the dramatic increase in the proportion of children growing up in fatherless households, and (2) the rise of the modern welfare state." (Rev. Robert A. Sirico, "Transforming the Culture of Fatherlessness" [http://www.acton.org/ppolicy/education/parent/fatherlessness.html].)

48   "Among communities dominated by the welfare system, fatherlessness is rampant. Today, fully 90 percent of U.S. families receiving cash welfare from government are without a father in the home. The very sociology of public welfare entails disincentives to intact families. Welfare programs address primarily or exclusively the material needs of people, most often of women and their children. When women and children are provided for by the state, a traditional and natural role for a father is usurped, undermining a man's sense of place in the family. Women, too, may judge the state to be a more reliable supporter than a husband, and opt out of marriage altogether. Both of these possibilities are indeed actualized under a regime of public welfare" (*Ibid.*)

49   "Moreover, the law's emphasis on moving mothers from welfare to work, although a good first step, does not

guarantee positive outcomes for children. Research shows that children do best when their families achieve increased employment and income, when they live in low-conflict households with the love and support of both parents…" ("Children and Welfare Reform: Executive Summary" from *The Future of Children*. [The Woodrow Wilson School of Public and International Affairs at Princeton University and The Brookings Institution. See http://www.futureofchildren.org/information3134/information_show.htm?doc_id=102726].)

50   "In a longitudinal study of 1,197 fourth-grade students, researchers observed 'greater levels of aggression in boys from mother-only households than from boys in mother-father households.'" (N. Vaden-Kierman, N. Ialongo, J. Pearson, and S. Kellam, "Household Family Structure and Children's Aggressive Behavior: A Longitudinal Study of Urban Elementary School Children," *Journal of Abnormal Child Psychology* 23, no. 5 [1995], quoted on http://www.photius.com/feminocracy/facts_on_fatherless_kids.html.) This is only one of many studies conducted on the results of fatherlessness on both boys and girls—results that include depression, violence, teen pregnancy, drug abuse, and suicide.

51   Letter from Abigail Adams to John Adams, October 16, 1774 (http://www.masshist.org/DIGITALADAMS/aea/cfm/doc.cfm?id=L17741016aa).

52   Letter from Abigail Adams to John Adams, August 29, 1776 (http://www.masshist.org/DIGITALADAMS/aea/cfm/doc.cfm?id=L17760829aa).

53   Refers to a quote by radical feminist Andrea Dworkin, "I'm a radical feminist, not the fun kind." "Dworkin

on Dworkin," an interview originally published in *Off Our Backs*, reprinted in *Radically Speaking: Feminism Reclaimed* (Melbourne, Australia: Spinifex Press, 1996), edited by Renate Klein and Diane Bell.

54   Paul W. Felix, "The Hermeneutics of Evangelical Feminism" in *The Master's Perspective on Contemporary Issues*, edited by Robert Thomas. (Grand Rapids, Michigan: Kregal, 1998).

55   *Ibid.*

56   Mary A. Kassian, *Women, Creation and the Fall* (Westchester, IL: Crossway, 1990), p. 147.

57   Wayne Grudem, *Evangelical Feminism: A New Path to Liberalism.* (Wheaton, IL: Crossway, 2006), p. 43. Hereafter cited as *Evangelical Feminism.*

58   *Finally Feminist*, pp. 51, 56-62 and 81.

59   The term patriarchy means "father-rule." Weldon Hardenbrook defines patriarchy as follows: "The biblical term patriarchy is derived from two words in the Greek language—patria (from the word pater, 'father'), which means 'family' or 'lineage'; and arches, which means 'ruler' or 'leader.' A patriarch is a family ruler. He is the man in charge." See Weldon Hardenbook, *Missing in Action: Vanishing Manhood in America* (Nashville: Thomas Nelson Publisher, 1987), p. 207.

60   *Finally Feminist*, pp. 57-58.

61   David L. Thompson, "Women, Men, Slaves, and the Bible: Hermeneutical Inquiries" in *Christian Scholar's Review* 25/3 (March 1996), pp. 326-349.

62   *Evangelical Feminism*, p. 347.

63   Matthew Henry, *Matthew Henry's Commentary on the Whole Bible: Complete and Unabridged in One Volume*, edited by Peabody Hendrickson, Libronix Digital Library, 1996, (1991), see 1 Peter 3:1.

64   Elisabeth Elliot, "The Essence of Femininity: A Personal Perspective" in *Recovering Biblical Manhood and Womanhood: A Response to Evangelical Feminism* (Wheaton, IL: Crossway Books, 1991).

65   It is important to note that a woman with an unrepentant, physically abusive husband should go to her elders for counsel, and in some cases to the civil authorities. A man abusing his family must be held to account by the authorities in his own life.

66   Matthew Henry, *The Quest for Meekness and Quietness of Spirit* (Morgan, PA: Soli Deo Gloria Publications, 1996). Hereafter cited as *Meekness and Quietness*.

67   Joseph Thayer, *Thayer's Greek-English Lexicon of the New Testament: Coded with Strong's Concordance Numbers* (Hendrickson Publishers, June 1, 1996, Rei Sub Edition).

68   *Meekness and Quietness,* pp. 17-18.

69   *Ibid.*, pp. 85-86.

70   Mary Kelley, *Woman's Being, Woman's Place* (Boston: G.K. Hall, 1979), pp. 240-241.

71   "Let your women keep silence in the churches: for it is not permitted unto them to speak; but they are commanded to be under obedience as also saith the law. And if they will learn any thing, let them ask their husbands at home: for it is a shame for women to speak in the church."

72   Brian Abshire, "Christian Education:

Should You Send Your Kids to College?"
(http://christian-civilization.org/shouldkidscollege.html)

73   Letter from Jane Austen to her niece, Fanny Knight,
written March 23, 1817. *Jane Austen's Letters*, collected and
edited by Deirdre Le Faye. (New York: Oxford University
Press, 1995), p. 335.

74   "Many Americans and Europeans are unaware of the
extremely low status that women, especially wives, had among
the ancient Athenians of Greece. A respectable Athenian
woman was not permitted to leave her house unless she was
accompanied by a trustworthy male escort, commonly a slave
appointed by her husband. When the husband's male guests
were present in his home, she was not permitted to eat or
interact with them. She had to retire to her woman's quarters
(*gynaeceum*). The only woman who had some freedom was
the *hetaera*, or mistress, who often accompanied a married
man when he attended events outside his home. The *hetaera*
was the man's companion and sexual partner...In addition
to depriving women of basic freedoms, Roman culture also
had an extremely low regard for women...The low regard for
women also showed itself in how they were used sexually...
[G]iven that sensuality in its most degrading forms pervaded
all classes...we find that promiscuous women were often
part of the pagan temple worship, for instance, in the temple
of Aphrodite. In the Roman and Greek temples sex was a
common religious activity. The pagan gods of the Romans
or Greeks set no precepts with regard to moral behavior."
(Alvin J. Schmidt, *How Christianity Changed the World*
[Grand Rapids: Zondervan, 2004], pp. 98, 101-102).